# NATIONAL WRITERS UNION
## GUIDE TO
# FREELANCE RATES & STANDARD PRACTICE

National Writers Union Guide to
Freelance Rates & Standard Practice

*Publisher:*
National Writers Union

*Distributors to the trade in the
United States and Canada:*
Writer's Digest Books
An imprint of F&W Publications, Inc.
1507 Dana Avenue
Cincinnati, OH 45207
1-800-289-0963

*Direct Mail Distribution:*
National Writers Union
873 Broadway   Suite 203
New York, NY 10003
phone: (212) 254-0279
fax: (212) 254-0673
e-mail: NWU@netcom.com

*Typesetting/Production:*
Kathryn Shagas Design
Brushwood Graphics, Inc.

*Printing:*
Peake Printers, Inc.
Pavsner Press, Inc.

printed and bound in the United States of America

*The National Writers Union
(NWU) is a 4,000-member union
of freelance writers—journalists,
book authors, poets, technical
writers, academic writers, and
many others—with twelve local
chapters throughout the United
States. The union is committed
to protecting the rights and
improving the economic conditions of freelance writers. It is
a local of the United Auto
Workers.*

# NATIONAL WRITERS UNION
## GUIDE TO
# FREELANCE RATES & STANDARD PRACTICE

Alexander Kopelman, *Writer/Editor*

Kathryn Shagas, *Designer*

Judith Levine, *Project Director*

# Contents

KEY:

WRITING LIFE

REFERENCE

NWU RECOMMENDS

WARNING!

## Acknowledgments

This book is a true product of collective labor. Special thanks go to the UAW for its support of the project and to the following people for their contributions:

Eleanor Arnason, Steve Askin, Margaret Bald, Paul Basista, Dan Baum, Barbara Beckwith, Peter Benjaminson, Maury Breecher, Judith Broadhurst, Michael Broder, Rachel Burd, Stanley Burnshaw, Debra Cash, Robert Chatelle, Ben Cheever, Linda Chester, Jesse Cohen, Marsha Cohen, Francisco Conde, Judith Cooper, Lee Cuba, Richard Curtis, Julie Kushner, Marcy Darnovsky, Peter Davidson, Lisa Duggan, Julie & Richard Farkas, Diana Finch, Carla Fine, Steve Fishman, Pete Fisk, Steve Fraser, Frank Free, Peter Frich, Sara Friedman, Barbara Garson, Jenevra Georgini, David Goodman, Ann Greiner, Robert Hambrecht, Bruce Hartford, Brett Harvey, Marc Hequet, Ed Hedemann, Lon Hide, Karla Huebner, Janet Jacobs, Beverly Jacobson, Lawrence Jacobson, Ron Johnson, Judy Jorgensen, John Justice, Judith Levine, David Lida, Priscilla Long, Arlene Lopez, Tony Machowski, Joel Makower, Philip Mattera, Virginia McCullough, Russell Miller, Anne Mitchell, Mary Mooney, Irvin Muchnick, Maria Pallante, Dean Paton, Jonathan Post, Amy Randall, Bob Reiser, Nita Renfrew, George Robinson, Martha Roth, Amy Rothman, Vanda Sendzimir, Karl Shmavonian, Stephen Simurda, Nancy DuVergne Smith, Sandra Storey, Alice Sunshine, Anna Szterenfeld, Jonathan Tasini, Andrea Thompson, Keith Watson, Janet Van Wicklen, Carole Vance, Ken Wolf, Steve Wolf, Sybil Wong, Nancy Yost, and Harry Youtt.

# Foreword

Iremember vividly the frustration I felt when I started my professional writing career more than a dozen years ago. Not from writer's block or recalcitrant sources. No—I was amazed, and often angry, at the lack of basic standards in the industry, from the absence of written contracts to wildly differing fees within the same publication.

The problem was exacerbated, I discovered quickly, by the dearth of information. Because most of us work in isolation, at home or in small offices, we don't share a water cooler, a physical space where we exchange the knowledge we accumulate about our working conditions. I probably survived because I was lucky enough to find the National Writers Union, a community of writers willing to share vital information, despite the competitiveness of our business.

Now that I am president of the NWU, I understand that our mission—to empower working writers to improve their lot, economically and politically—has to extend beyond our own ranks. As we face a new era, in which our work can be whisked around the globe in the blink of an eye by an industry bearing little resemblance to the publishing world of the past, we must find ways to communicate with each other and work together to hold back the tide of worsening economic conditions for all writers. The first step in that direction is to educate as many writers as we can about the nuts and bolts of the freelance markets.

The book you hold is unique. Based on an independent survey, it is the collective wisdom of writers like you. Unlike other writers' guides, it does not present only what publishers say they do, but what we know to be the real facts of our daily work lives—and what the union believes those facts should be.

The inspiration for the book came from NWU activists in Boston. Several years ago, the Boston Journalists Committee produced a regional New England guide for writers. When a copy showed up in the union's national office, it was obvious to me that a national guide would be invaluable to thousands of writers throughout the country.

You will see many names throughout the pages of the book: union members who gave their time and thought to help make it easier for every writer to earn a living wage and not go crazy doing it. Many thanks also go to the United Auto Workers, our parent organization, for its significant support for the project.

So go forth with this information and rake in the dough. Let us know what you think and what might be helpful for future editions.

Most important, remember one thing. While this guide will certainly help give the straight dope on the real world, the only true solution to empowering every writer is through common and united action. So, consider this a personal invitation to join the National Writers Union.

# Introduction

Writing is a difficult business. As writers, we struggle with self-doubt, fear of exposure, rejection, isolation, writer's block, and a host of other psychological hobgoblins. But as difficult as the emotions of writing are, most freelance writers will agree that the toughest thing about writing is making a living from our craft.

We are not talking about getting assignments and getting published. Even many full-time working freelance writers have a hard time paying their bills with what they earn from writing alone. In the National Writers Union survey, we found that only slightly over 50 percent of responding writers had annual freelance incomes of more than $10,000. And these are not novice writers: close to 85 percent described their careers as "established" or "moderately established."

Why are writers so bad off? The reasons are complex and varied—from recession and industry consolidation to poor distribution systems and shrinking demand. The underlying reason for freelance writers' economic plight, however, remains our relationship with publishers and other organizations that hire us.

This relationship is defined by two interconnected factors: the absence of minimum standards for compensation and working conditions; and a profound power imbalance between writers and publishers. (*Note:* For the sake of convenience, *publisher* is used to mean "anyone who hires writers" and *freelancer* to mean "any independently employed writer.")

## Writers and Publishers

Samuel Johnson once said that "no man but a blockhead ever wrote except for money." His sentiment is in direct opposition to the widespread image of the writer as a gaunt artist pounding away at the keyboard in blind dedication to the craft, oblivious to cold, hunger, and all other adversity. This metaphor of writing as a self-sacrificing search for meaning and self-expression is deeply rooted in our culture and in the hearts of many writers.

The metaphor is certainly flattering, since it communicates the discipline and commitment required of a writer. But it is also deceptive and dangerous, because it perpetuates the view of writing as the fulfillment of one's creative urge, not a labor for which one gets paid.

*The image of the starving artist is flattering— but it perpetuates the idea that writing isn't gainful employment*

This conception is, in part, responsible for the imbalance of power that exists between writers and publishers. Many writers consider themselves lucky to be published, regardless of how well they get paid, or in some cases whether they get paid at all. We fear and loathe rejection, and when someone likes our work enough to pay us for it, we dare not risk alienating him or her by asking for a higher fee or a better contract.

Publishers, on the other hand, are not emotionally invested in the business. Their primary goal is to maximize profits, and the best way to do that is to minimize costs. Take the example of a hardcover book. After discounts, a publisher can expect to get approximately $10 in gross revenue from a trade book with a list price of $19.95. Out of that, about $1.75 goes for manufacturing, $1.50 for production, $2.50 for overhead, and $2.50 for author royalties of 10 percent to 15 percent of list price. The publisher is left with a profit of $1.75.

Now let's say the publisher pays the author a royalty of 10 percent to 15 percent on publisher's net—it is common for publishers to pay royalties on the amount actually received after discounts rather than on the cover price of the book—the royalty is reduced to about $1.25, and the publisher's profit increases to $3.[1] Simple arithmetic: It is in the publisher's best interest to pay the author as little as possible.

[1] Calculations based on figures provided in Standard & Poor's Industry Surveys: Media. February 11, 1993.

This is not to say that publishers are mean, greedy people who live to cheat starving writers out of decent pay. They are, for the most part, honest people doing their jobs—acquiring the best possible writing at the lowest possible price.

The relationship between writer and publisher is thus innately problematic, since it pits the interests of an individual against those of a corporate structure. Although these interests coincide to a certain degree, they are vastly different and are, in fact, at odds in some respects. And the corporation, with its large financial and human resources, is invariably in a better position to protect its interests.

The problem is exacerbated by the fact that many writers feel uncomfortable with the business of writing—setting and negotiating fees, reviewing contracts, selling rights, and so on. By shying away from these issues, we often leave the decisions about how much we get paid and on what conditions to the publishers. Not surprisingly, the compensation and conditions we are given are frequently not in our favor.

*Writers must take off the artist's jeans and put on the businessperson's starched collar*

To correct this imbalance of power, it is incumbent on each of us to become our own business manager. We need to learn to step out of the role of writer—with its solitary labor, intense thought, and torn jeans—and into the role of entrepreneur—with its contracts, negotiations, and starched collars. Until writers stand together and take an active, equal part in setting compensation rates and determining working conditions, we cannot hope to improve our economic and professional lives.

Also, we believe, writers need a union, in which they can work collectively to make their individual lots better.

## Standards

"Fine," you say, "I am willing to roll up my sleeves and negotiate, but how do I know what value my work has in the marketplace?" That is where we come to the question of standards.

How *do* we know what our work is worth and what are acceptable conditions? Each of us can determine what he or she needs to earn every month. We can say what we would like to get paid for a particular piece. Some of us can even tell which rights we want to sell and which to keep. But most of this is guesswork, and more often then not we end up accepting the publisher's "standard."

The fact of the matter is that there are few standards in the industry. Even individual publishers rarely have standards for rates paid to freelance writers. Rates are set more or less arbitrarily on a case-by-case basis. Many journalists, for example, have had the experience of doing a story very similar to one they had done for the same editor six months earlier, only to find that the fee is less than what they got the first time.

It is, in a way, paradoxical even to speak of a freelance writing industry, much less of industry standards. We freelancers produce such diverse creations as romance novels, software manuals, political speeches, poems, newspaper and magazine articles, and textbooks. And the organizations that employ us to write range from the huge media conglomerates that own a great many consumer magazines and publishing houses to literary magazines with shoe-string budgets, large foundations, small electronics manufacturers, and government agencies.

It is, of course, impossible to develop uniform standards for such a broad range of economic activity. However, it is quite possible to look at the industry as a collection of individual genre markets and to begin to articulate standards for each of these markets.

This book does precisely that: It gives writers in the six major freelance markets identified by the NWU—journalism, book writing, technical writing, corporate/nonprofit communications, writing for literary magazines, and academic writing—benchmarks by which to judge the value of their work in the marketplace and the working conditions afforded by their contracts.

## About This Guide

The National Writers Union conceived this book in response to the almost complete lack of reliable, current information about freelance writing rates and practices. To collect this information, the NWU, with assistance from faculty of the Sociology Department at Wellesley College, conducted a large-scale survey of American writers. More than 1,200 writers, working in all of the six major genres, participated by completing detailed questionnaires about earnings, working conditions, rates and practices in specific genres, and other professional and economic issues. The results of the survey, augmented by data gathered by other organizations, as well as interviews with editors, agents, and publishers, are at the heart of this book.

The book is written by working writers for working writers. It is not meant to be a manual on how to become a professional writer, but rather a reference tool for professional writers who want to improve their economic conditions.

The book is designed to be flexible and accessible. If you want to find the going rate for, let's say, a press release for a nonprofit organization, you can refer directly to a rate chart for corporate/nonprofit communications. And if you then want to find out more about setting fees and negotiating contracts, you can read a couple of sections in the appropriate chapters.

There are four parts to the book: *Rights & Responsibilities, The Markets, The Politics of Writing,* and *About the Union.*

*Rights and Responsibilities* consists of four chapters—"Rates & Working Conditions," "Rights," "Contracts," and "The Electronic Future: New Rules for New Media"—that cover business and professional issues of interest to all writers.

*The Markets* focuses on six of the genres: *Journalism, Books, Technical Writing, Corporate/Nonprofit Communications, Literary Magazines,* and *Academic Writing.* The presentation in each consists of a graphic display of rate and practice information for the particular genre—accompanied by NWU suggested standards—and a detailed discussion of the specific issues and problems that face writers in the genre.

## THE SURVEY

The purpose of the NWU survey was to begin to develop a picture, where previously there was practically none, of the economic conditions and industry practices under which writers work. We also saw the survey as an opportunity to hear from writers themselves about their working lives.

The data we gathered from the more than 1,200 writers who participated have two distinctive characteristics: They show a remarkable degree of variance in the pay rates in most genres and indicate a marked lack of understanding on the part of many writers of such business basics as contracts and rights.

*The Politics of Writing* offers a discussion of censorship, and discrimination in the industry.

*About the Union* gives an overview of the National Writers Union—its history, philosophy, and the services it provides to its members.

Although this book is addressed primarily to writers, it is our hope that everyone who hires writers will also find it useful in negotiating fair contracts and compensation. Equitable, professional standards in all freelance markets will help writers and publishers work closer together to bring forth better brochures, poems, manuals, books, articles—better writing—in a more just industry.

*1*

*Rights & Responsibilities*

# Rates & Working Conditions

To say that writers, as a group, are underpaid is a grotesque understatement. The fact is that most of us cannot survive on what we earn from writing, despite the attention that the select few receive with million-dollar contracts. The median annual freelance writing income for those who participated in NWU research was between $6,000 and $10,000. In other words, the representative writer earns no more than $10,000 a year. Close to 30 percent of writers had incomes of under $2,000, and only the top 15 percent earned over $30,000 per year.

The numbers are chilling enough in themselves. However, if we look at the change in writers' incomes over the years, things look even more bleak. The Survey of American Authors[1] found that the median writing income in the United States in 1979 was $4,775. As you can see, we have made very little progress. And given the fact that the cost of living has increased 150 percent in the last ten years alone, we have taken a step backward.

*The median writer's income is $10,000 a year, and only 15 percent make more than $30,000*

This becomes even clearer when we consider writers' income as a function of hourly pay. The estimated median hourly wage—based on the average amount of time spent on writing—of the writers who participated in our research was $5.33. A comparable estimate puts the 1979 figure at $4.90.[2]

Non-staff writers make $1.07 more an hour than the national minimum wage. In other words, people who shape the intellectual climate of the United States, who on average have been committed to their profession for 15 years, and 84 percent of whom consider them-

---

[1] Conducted by The Authors Guild Foundation and Columbia University Center for Social Studies. Kingston, P.W. and J.R. Cole, 1986. *The Wages of Writing*. Columbia University Press, New York.
[2] Ibid.

selves "established" or "moderately established" in their careers are in economic terms slightly above the poverty line.

Staff writers fare somewhat better: The median income for this group—which comprises magazine, corporate communications, and technical writers—is $25,000, or approximately $12.50 an hour. This too, of course, is significantly lower than what writers should earn.

What this fact says about our society is beyond the scope of this book. What it says about the need for immediate action is clear: Unless we writers raise our voices and our pens to demand that our contribution to the economy of this country be recognized and remunerated, we will continue to struggle at minimum wage only to subsidize the profits of the corporations that publish our work.

## Rates

In a free-market economy, value is determined, at least in principle, by market demand. But what is a writer's market—the book publishers, periodicals, and corporations who pay us to use our work or the people who read that work? The relationship is complex, but in general writers do not have direct access to their primary market (except in genres such as technical writing and corporate/nonprofit communications).

The economic value of writers' work is for the most part determined by publishers. Since these entities tend to be corporations, their primary motivation is not personal desire but profit. The calculus is simple: Publishers want to get writing that will appeal to the greatest number of readers at the lowest possible price. For writers this translates into near-minimum-wage pay rates.

But what can you do about this? First of all, throw out the notion that writers are powerless. We have to see ourselves as "workers in words," to paraphrase Leonard Cohen. And as workers we have to demand fair, consistent standards of payment.

Although each of us may work in solitude, none of us is alone. Freelance writers are a power, both economic and social. So every time an individual writer asks for better pay, we are all standing up for our rights.

The bottom line is: Writers deserve to make a living wage from writing.

## *Working Conditions*

How much we get paid for our labor is important, but it is not the only issue. The working conditions prevalent in individual genres and in the industry as a whole are also of vital interest. Such common practices as kill fees, blanket indemnification clauses, long delays in payment, seizure of copyright, and lack of editorial control adversely affect our professional lives on a regular basis. Reasonable, consistent standards need to be implemented to address these issues, as well.

# Rights

Legal rights in our work and the ability to sell and license these rights are at the foundation of writers' economic lives. To empower ourselves professionally and financially, we must understand the basic principles of the laws that grant us these rights, as well as the mechanisms for capitalizing on the rights. In this chapter, we will look at the concept of copyright and at the rights derived from it.

## Copyright

U.S. copyright law is based on a constitutional clause that empowers the Congress to foster creative labor "by securing for limited times to authors . . . the exclusive right to their respective writings . . . ."[1] The law thus essentially defines a writer's work as *property* that the author owns. This definition casts the relationship between writers and their works as an economic one, and the law is designed to safeguard an author's ability to profit from creative work by giving the author a monopoly over the work in the form of five exclusive rights to exploit the work for financial gain.

### WORKS ELIGIBLE FOR COPYRIGHT

The Copyright Act of 1976 grants legal protection to "original works of authorship." What is an original work of authorship? Anything you *write*—that is, create, rather than find or copy. For example, if you discover documentary evidence that J.F.K.'s assassination was indeed a high-level government conspiracy and publish a book based on this evidence, you will own the copyright to the book you write but not to the facts you discover.

---

[1]U.S. Constitution, Article I, Section 8, Clause 8.

*We will take a closer look at the question of copyright and electronic publishing in "The Electronic Future: New Rules," page 21.*

To qualify for copyright protection, the work must be "fixed in any tangible medium of expression, now known or later developed." In other words, a poem you write on a cocktail napkin is eligible for copyright; one you write in the snow outside your lover's window is not. **The issue of medium becomes particularly important as we move further into the electronic age.**

## THE EXCLUSIVE RIGHTS

The current Copyright Act grants the owner of a copyright the exclusive right:

1. To make copies of the copyrighted work. This means that no one is allowed to reproduce your work, in any form, without your permission. (There are some exceptions under the "fair use" doctrine which we will discuss a bit later.)

2. To develop derivative works based on the copyrighted material. To put this simply, a movie producer cannot make a film based on your book *Lab of My Life* without your consent.

3. To sell, rent, lease, or lend copies of the copyrighted work to the public. In other words, you have complete control over the life of your work and its exposure to the public.

4. To perform the copyrighted work publicly. Without your permission, no one can read from your work to an audience.

5. To display the copyrighted work publicly. Unless you agree to it, your poems cannot be plastered on billboards along the information superhighway.

As of this writing, the right to transmit one's work is very likely to be added to this list as the sixth exclusive right.

*The copyright always belongs to you—unless you sign it away*

All of this amounts to one point: You, the author, have a legal monopoly in your work.

The law, however, also provides that the author has the right to dispose of each individual exclusive right as he or she wishes. You can sell, lease, rent, license, or give away any one of the rights. This makes it possible to sell various rights to the same copyrighted work to different buyers, thus greatly increasing your income from the work. For example, you can sell the right to publish your book to hardcover, paperback, or CD-ROM publishers, the right to print excerpts from the book to a magazine, and the right to make a movie based on the book to a film studio. The only condition governing the transfer of exclusive rights is that it be done in writing.

## INFRINGEMENT

Any violation of the five exclusive rights, except those specifically exempted in the Copyright Act and those designated "fair use," is an infringement of the copyright. For instance, if someone were to print and sell copies of your book without your permission, that would be an infringement. On the other hand, the copyright would not be infringed if someone bought a copy of the same book from a book-store and then resold it.

Copyright infringement is punished in a variety of ways. A court may issue an injunction against the infringer, thus putting an end to the offending activity. It may order the publication or use to cease. All profits from the infringement may be awarded to the owner of the copyright. The copyright holder may also be awarded monetary damages and lawyers' fees. Even criminal charges may be filed against the infringer in some instances.

Despite the law's dim view of copyright violation, however, infringement is not always easy to prove and is usually debated in each individual case. Particularly murky and difficult are issues of "fair use."

## FAIR USE

The concept of "fair use" is rather ungainly. The idea is that the use of copyrighted material without the consent of the copyright holder should be permitted for certain purposes that advance the greater general good, such as education and news reporting.

This principle was codified into a statute for the first time in the Copyright Act of 1976. The Act states that "the fair use of a copyrighted work...for purposes such as criticism, comment, news reporting, teaching (including multiple copies for classroom use), scholarship, or research, is not an infringement of copyright."

The Act also provides four factors to be used in determining fair use:

- *The purpose and character of the use.* This consideration is designed to determine whether the user is likely to make money from the unauthorized use of the copyrighted material without paying its owner. For example, if a teacher makes copies of an essay of yours and distributes them to her students, this will likely be considered fair use. On the other hand, if she *charges* the students for the essay, she is unfairly infringing on your copyright.

- *The nature of the copyrighted work.* A scholarly article, for instance, is more likely to be used "fairly" than an erotic short story. The material lends itself to commentary and study by others. Out-of-print works are more likely to be the objects of "fair" unauthorized use, while unpublished works can almost never be used in this way.

- *The amount and substantiality of the portion used.* In other words, how much and what is taken. Several paragraphs from an essay may be considered fair use, while a couple of lines from a poem may be seen as an infringement. There are no definitive guidelines for this. Of course, the more that is taken, the less "fair" is the use.

- *The effect of the use upon the potential market for or value of the copyrighted work.* This means that if, by scanning your pamphlet "Twenty-five Survival Tips for College Freshmen" into his college's computer network, a dean undermined your ability to sell the pamphlet on campus, the use would be considered an infringement of your copyright. The economic impact is the most important consideration in determining fair use.

**W**ARNING!

Questions of fair use are important to writers not only in protecting our own work but also in using the work of others. **As fellow authors, we should be particularly careful to make *fair use* of each other's writing.**

## REGISTRATION AND TERM OF COPYRIGHT

Your work is protected by copyright law regardless of whether or not it is registered with the Copyright Office. A work, however, must be registered before an infringement suit can be brought to court. (The work can be registered after an infringement has been discovered.)

Copyright protection extends for the life of the owner plus 50 years. In cases of joint ownership, the term of copyright is the life of the last surviving owner plus 50 years. The term of copyright in the United States is likely to be extended to the life of the owner plus 70 years in the near future, to reflect changes that have taken place in much of the rest of the world.

## COPYRIGHT OWNERSHIP

The law is very clear on this point: **Copyright belongs to the author of the work.**

There is an important exception to this rule. The copyright of "works made for hire" belongs to the writer's employer or the commissioning party.

There are also works of authorship that cannot be copyrighted at all, notably most titles and short phrases and any U.S. government documents.

## WORK FOR HIRE

It is very important that writers understand the concept of "work made for hire"—or as it is frequently called, "work for hire." "Work-for-hire" contracts are standard in such genres as technical writing and corporate/nonprofit communications, and are cropping up with alarming frequency in journalism, book writing, and other markets. You need to know when such a contract is appropriate and when it represents an exploitative attempt by the publisher to seize the copyright to your work.

Two types of work made for hire are recognized by the Copyright Act of 1976.

■ ***Work prepared by an employee within the scope of his or her employment.*** In other words, the copyright to the 200-page report on the adverse effects of noise on the reproduction rates of pere-grine falcons in New York City, which you wrote as part of your job, belongs to the environmental organization where you work.

It is important to note that employment is defined by such factors as where you work, at home or in the employer's office, whose equipment you use, and who pays your social security.

■ *Work specially ordered or commissioned.* Although this sounds simple enough, there are actually a number of rather complex factors that define a commissioned work as a work made for hire.

◆ The types of work that can be made for hire are limited by the law to: "a contribution to a collective work…translation …supplementary work…compilation…instructional text… test…answer material for a test." Under this limitation, works for hire are usually magazine articles, book chapters, or some other contributions to larger works. Books, unless they are intended to be used as material for "systematic instruction," are usually not considered works for hire.

◆ The work must be clearly commissioned; its creation must be motivated by the publisher or employer. For instance, if a computer software corporation approaches you to write a user manual, it is commissioning a work made for hire on the grounds that the work is a supplementary text. On the other hand, if the same corporation includes in its product documentation an article you had previously written about its software, the article can in no way be considered a work made for hire.

**WARNING!**
**Cross out any work-for-hire statements on checks.**

Finally, a written agreement between the writer and the employer must expressly specify that the work is made for hire. There is some confusion about when such agreements have to be signed, because the law does not address that issue. Some publishers include work-for-hire agreement language above the endorsement on writers' checks. Some go further by requiring writers to sign agreements that all work they do for that publisher will be work for hire. Since in a work-for-hire agreement you are forfeiting your copyright, be careful about entering such agreements. Cross out any work-for-hire statements on checks. And certainly try to avoid blanket agreements.

## Selling Rights

Copyright is one of the most precious possessions a writer has. From it derive the rights to our work which we sell, lease, and license to earn our living. Clearly, copyright is not a possession to be given away lightly. Many writers, unfortunately, let themselves be intimidated into relinquishing the copyright to their work.

Of course, holding on to the copyright of some types of work makes no sense since the sub-rights are virtually impossible to exploit. For instance, it is highly improbable that you could sell movie rights to an instructional manual for a forklift. On the other hand, signing over the copyright to a magazine article about propane poisoning among forklift operators might deprive you of the income from a potential television deal.

In general, **unless you are fairly certain that you cannot derive any additional benefits from the copyright, do not sign over the copyright to your work.**

What about the rights derived from the copyright? How do you know which ones to sell and which ones to keep? As a rule, the more single-purpose rights you can sell, the more money you can make from your work. For example, if in the agreement with the publisher of your most recent book, *Stories on Tap: A Winter in the Bars of Alaska*, you grant the publisher the merchandising rights, along with hardcover and paperback rights, you have to share the profits from the hot-selling caps, t-shirts, and jackets with the publisher. If you sell the merchandising rights directly to the company producing the caps, etc., however, you get to keep all of the money.

The issues surrounding rights are very different in each of the genre markets. For book authors, for instance, there are complex questions about subsidiary rights. For academic writers there are questions of copyright. We will look at the specific issues in detail in the sections that deal with each genre individually.

In general, when negotiating the grant of rights, consider what you might want to do with the work, what is possible, and who is best equipped to handle particular rights. The bottom line should always be how you can profit most from your work.

NWU
RECOMMENDS

*For more on specific rights, see Part 2: The Markets.*

# Contracts

Generally, when people think of contracts, we imagine devilish documents—pages and pages of ponderous legalese in triplicate—that are as likely as not to have us sign away our first-born children *and* to land us in court. Writers, in particular, seem to have an aversion to contracts. Maybe it is because the existence of a contract underlines the economic aspects of our profession, or maybe we are reluctant to ask for the conditions we want. Whatever the case, a great many writers either work without contracts or do not pay attention to the contracts they do sign.

This, to put it mildly, is imprudent. Contracts can and must be tools that help secure the compensation and working conditions we need and protect our rights. To have contracts perform this role, writers have to understand the basics about contracts, their purpose, and scope.

In this chapter, we will take a look at what contracts are, how to negotiate them, what to do in case of a dispute, and where to look for help.

## It's a Contract!

### THE THEORY

Strictly speaking, any deal—or even an understanding—between two people is a contract, as long as it can be enforced by law. It does not matter whether the agreement is written or verbal. To be considered a binding legal contract, though, an agreement must represent a promise by each person entering the agreement to do something and an acceptance of each promise by the other.

An example will help. Let's say you want to write a service article on dogs, "Teaching an Old Dog to Swim." You send a query to an editor you know at *Dog Fancy*. You and the editor talk things over and agree that you and she want to do business together. That, in itself, is not a contract. Then she offers to pay you $1,200 for a 1,000-word piece; you accept and promise to deliver the story in three months. You now have a contract, at least in theory.

### THE REALITY

Now, let's look at real life. For writers, in particular, anything but a written contract is not worth the paper it is printed on. Verbal contracts are extremely difficult to enforce and therefore provide little legal protection.

*Anything but a written contract isn't worth the paper it's printed on*

In fact, the law requires written contracts in many instances. For example, throughout the U.S., any agreement involving a task that will take longer than a year to complete—the writing of a book, for instance—must be made in writing to be binding. In many parts of the country, written contracts are required if any money is at stake.

Most important for writers, the U.S. Copyright Act demands a written agreement in instances where the owner of a copyrighted work grants exclusive rights in that work or transfers the copyright itself to another person (or organization).

## Content

A contract should describe as explicitly and fully as possible all aspects of the agreement. The rights and obligations of each party are particularly important.

The contracts freelance writers deal with vary tremendously, as you might expect. At one extreme are the complex documents prevalent among book publishers; at the other are assignment-confirmation letters used by many freelance journalists. There are some basic elements, however, that all writing contracts should contain, at minimum.

- *Scope of work:* A contract should always contain a detailed description of the work to be created, including content, editorial direction, and estimated length.

*For a detailed discussion of copyright and publishing rights, see "Rights," page 7.*

- **Rights:** The copyright of a work is by definition the property of the work's creator. It allows the author to sell individual publishing rights in the work. A contract should make it clear which publishing rights you are granting to the publisher, in what geographical area, and for how long.

  **Beware contracts that seek to strip you of your copyright.**

**WARNING!**

- **Fees:** The financial arrangement should be spelled out as fully as possible. This might include fees, royalties, advances, payment schedules, expenses, fees for additional work, and so on.

- **Time frame:** All deadlines have to be spelled out, along with procedures for extending deadlines.

- **Legal responsibility:** The contract should make clear the role and responsibility of each party in the event a claim or suit arises as a result of the work.

  **The NWU strongly urges writers to try not to accept without amendment contracts that contain blanket indemnification clauses— provisions that place complete financial responsibility on the writer in case of a suit.**

*For suggestions on amending indemnification clauses see page 77.*

- **Termination:** The contract must clearly state the conditions under which the parties can break the agreement.

- **Disputes:** A procedure for settling disputes between the author and the publisher should be delineated by the contract. It is a good idea to have arbitration specified as the primary method for resolving problems.

*For more on arbitration, see pages 19, 36, and 78.*

# Negotiating

In some cultures, it is considered rude not to bargain at the market-place. In others, it is looked on as simply foolish. In the United States, of course, we are not used to haggling; it is generally hard to get the manager of your local supermarket to come down on the price of frozen peas. But even in this culture, no self-respecting business person accepts the first bid offered.

Writers, unfortunately, tend to feel uncomfortable with the idea of negotiating. Many of us approach our business with the fear that if we ask for a higher fee, better terms, or even more reasonable conditions, we will simply be passed up for the next writer in line. As a negotiating posture, this attitude leaves a lot to be desired.

The crucial thing to remember is that the moment when a publisher (or any other client) offers you a contract is the pinnacle of your power in the relationship. The publisher is in effect saying that you have something he or she wants.

If you see the situation this way, you begin to realize that you are in a position to discuss, and to a certain degree dictate, the conditions under which you would be willing to satisfy the publisher's wish. At this point, a dialogue can begin.

*The NWU's Standard Journalism Contract is on page 61.*

Ideally, you would open the discussion by presenting the publisher with your conditions in the form of a written contract. It is fairly rare in most freelance markets, however, for the writer to be the one to furnish the contract.

It is usually the publisher who provides the contract. Most such contracts are written to serve as starting points for negotiations. They are, to one degree or another, boilerplate—language that generalizes terms common in the marketplace. There are, of course, certain points that are nonnegotiable, but you can at least talk about making changes to most clauses.

Negotiating does not have to be bellicose. A lot can be accomplished through a calm exchange of positions, wishes, and needs. It is rarely necessary to come to blows, although banging your shoe on the table can sometimes be effective.

The real trick to negotiating is a carefully thought-out strategy. Consider what you want out of the deal. Then divide your wishes into categories based on desirability. For instance, you could look at the various provisions of a contract as: (1) the things you would like, but can give up without much pain; (2) the things you would give up only in exchange for something else; and (3) the things you absolutely cannot live without. You can then approach the negotiations with a series of demands and fall-back positions. The goal is to get as much of what you want as possible, but not to back the other party into a corner, where the only way out is to break off negotiations.

Finally, it is important to be realistic. Do not make wild demands, but be firm about asking for the things you want. By approaching negotiations in a professional, thoughtful way, you will make better deals.

# In Case of Trouble

It is a fact of life that relationships between writers and publishers sometimes sour. It is essential that your contracts make provisions for such contingencies.

The situation you want to avoid is one where a dispute has arisen and you are forced to give in because you do not have the resources to fight a legal battle. Independently employed writers, even successful ones, are generally unable to take on the organizations with which they have contracts. Therefore, negotiate hard to include an arbitration clause in your contract.

Arbitration is a binding means of settling disagreements that arise between parties to a contract. It is less expensive and quicker than litigation. The particular advantage of arbitration is that it counters some of the power imbalance between writers and publishers.

There are several respected arbitration services throughout the country. The best known of these is the American Arbitration Association.

# Contract Help

**The National Writers Union** offers members help in contractual matters through its Standard Journalism Contract, *NWU Guide to Book Contracts*, *NWU Preferred Literary Agent Agreement*, and other publications. The Union also provides expert advice and offers representation during arbitration.

*More on the Standard Journalism Contract: page 59.*

The NWU's grievance process is another valuable resource for members who need help in resolving contractual problems.

Other writer's organizations also offer publications and advice about contracts. Among them are: **American Society of Journalists and Authors, The Authors Guild, PEN American Center, Poets & Writers Inc.**

*Grievances: page 193.*

**Volunteer Lawyers for the Arts,** with branches throughout the country, provides free or affordable legal services to artists, depending on income.

# The Electronic Future: New Rules for New Media[1]

The more we look at the emerging information technologies, the clearer it becomes that we are in the midst of an information revolution as profound and far reaching as the one triggered by Gutenberg's printing press. The printing press was not just a more efficient hand-scribe; it totally transformed the way in which information was created, reproduced, sold, and consumed. It created information markets and formats undreamt of in the quill-pen universe, and it brought into being new economic institutions and relationships and altered old ones beyond recognition. We are about to experience a similar revolution, but instead of time measured in centuries, we will see this occur in a decade or less.

The computer networks of today are the forerunners of the world infosphere of tomorrow. This infosphere will provide intellectual property—information, art, and entertainment—on demand from a galaxy of public and private sources in a multitude of formats: written, visual, audio, and multimedia. For us as authors, the world infosphere will become an enormous electronic marketplace where commercial vendors, including ourselves, will transmit and sell the intellectual property that we create in a variety of formats.

*If writers don't speak up now, publishers and vendors will make the rules of the electronic marketplace*

It is crucial that writers participate in shaping the economic relationships and distribution patterns that these new technologies are creating. If we remain silent on the sidelines, the rules, practices, and customs of the new electronic marketplaces will be determined entirely by publishers and vendors for their benefit and not ours.

---

[1] This chapter is based on "Electronic Publishing Issues," an NWU working paper by Bruce Hartford and Jonathan Tasini.

# The Economics of Change

In the electronic marketplace, authors and artists will be able to sell a variety of electronic distribution rights in a variety of ways. For example:

- the right to read, view, or otherwise use, either restricted or unrestricted
- the right to make digital (electronic) copies, either restricted or unrestricted
- the right to redistribute the work to others
- all electronic distribution rights

An author or artist can be paid for these rights in a variety of ways. For example:

- per-use royalty
- lump sum
- time rental or time-access period
- income share

These fees can be paid on a variety of bases. For example:

- each user's access / use
- each machine's access / use
- site license

Negotiations and agreements for the sale and transfer of intellectual property have already grown more complicated and will become immeasurably more so in the future.

Although we cannot predict the exact shape the electronic marketplace will assume, the National Writers Union advocates the following principles:

- The copyright principle should be applied to the electronic marketplaces.
- Electronic rights are a subsidiary right, just like sales to a paperback publisher, book club, or movie company, and should be treated as such.

- Control over electronic rights—when, by whom, in what form, and for how much the work may be remade or redistributed electronically—should be retained by the author, and surrendered only for a fair payment.

- Payments for electronic rights should reflect the relative value added to the product by publisher and author. When books are sold and distributed electronically, the publisher has none of the traditional printing, binding, warehousing, shipping, and return costs. On the other side, the author often provides typesetting via desktop publishing, indexing, artwork, and so forth. Both facts point to the principle that authors should receive higher, not lower, fees and royalties for electronic rights.

- Work-for-hire contracts (the publisher, as "author" of the work, holds the copyrights) and all-rights contracts (all rights are transferred by the author to the publisher) for works intended for general mass publication are coercive and unfair. They are often used as subterfuges for gaining electronic distribution rights without payment. In this context, "general publication" is understood to include books, newspapers, magazines, and analogous electronic formats in which the main product purchased is the author's work.

- Work-for-hire and all-rights contracts are legitimate in situations where the author's words are an adjunct to what the customer is buying, such as technical manuals accompanying a product or a report describing the results of someone's research; or in which the author's work is not offered for sale directly to the public, as in the case of advertising copy, grant proposals, corporate newsletters, and so forth. Work-for-hire is also legitimate when work is prepared within the scope of someone's employment as part of his or her normal job duties. Thus, for example, when a staff reporter for a newspaper writes a story, the paper owns the copyright, not the reporter.

## *Public Interest in the Electronic Age*

The struggle for our economic interests in the electronic age must be seen in a broader context. The revolution we are witnessing will touch the lives of every person in society, dramatically altering the way in which we work, relax and interact with their co-workers, family, friends and neighbors. As the world changes, we must advance our agenda hand-in-hand with segments of society concerned about how the new information age will reshape our daily existence.

On the one hand, a significant segment of public interest groups are advancing the argument that information should be free, that new technologies will allow many more people to become creators of content, that copyright will not exist in the new information age because it will be too easy to pirate and distribute work without permission. This position endangers the livelihood of everyone engaged in creative work. As writers, we must participate in this discussion, praising the potential flood of new creators who will broaden and enrich our culture, but, at the same time, speaking up for our place as cultural treasures whose ability to survive must be protected.

In addition, we have to advocate for a truly universal system, to which all people, without regard to social or economic standing, have access. Universal access will not happen naturally despite the rhetoric of the so-called "information superhighway." Indeed, without a broad effort, we will end up with a system of toll roads where access to high-value material will be based on ability to pay. That will guarantee a society divided into information haves and information have-nots, in which we will be the purveyors of culture to a few.

## *The Government's Role*

**NWU RECOMMENDS**

The NWU also advocates that the following points be established through legislation or the regulatory process:

- When intellectual property is sold or electronically distributed across national boundaries, the copyright laws of the nation where the work was originally created should apply to that work.

- Authors should be free to retain any and all electronic distribution rights and should not be coerced into selling them. The practice of using a form on the back of a payment check to enumerate additional rights the author surrenders to the publisher by cashing the check should be illegal.

- Because you should not be coerced into giving up or selling rights not yet understood or conceived of, a grant of all rights should not include rights to media or technologies that do not exist at the time the grant is made.

- The interpretation of the "fair use" provision of the Copyright Act should take into account the need for unimpeded flow of information, while protecting the legitimate interests of those who own copyrights.

- When databases containing intellectual property are compiled, each piece of information should include the author's name and the rights to that piece of information that are owned by the author and publisher.

- Authors and the owners of intellectual property should have the right to encrypt their data to assure that their copyrights are not violated. The right of the people to encrypt their data by any means they choose should not be abridged, denied, or limited. We oppose legislation requiring hardware and software to contain trapdoors that governments can use to read encrypted information. No one shall be required to decrypt their data except through due process of law.

*The Markets*

2

# ABOUT OUR RECOMMENDATIONS

Setting standards is a tricky business, a balancing act between what's common market-place practice and what should be common, what seems immediately achievable with a little added aggression and what is a long shot, yet is perfectly fair, and therefore the right thing to recommend.

As the conditions of writers' working lives worsen, common practice—25 percent kill fees, blanket indemnification clauses, unpaid seizure of electronic rights—moves further from the perfectly fair, which in turn becomes less easily achievable. Even as we read in the papers about book advances in the seven figures, our survey turned up advances and royalty rates many New York literary agents would sneer at. At the same time, in spite of industry consolidation, the market is dividing into smaller and smaller segments. All of this makes it harder to zero in on one "correct" recommendation.

## Realism + Vision = Optimism

"Realism" might dictate recommending what most writers are usually getting. But we don't want to stand for something that is not as good as what some writers may achieve. Instead, the higher range of our recommendations are as high as anybody is currently likely to get. It's a mixture of realism and vision—call it optimism.

If some of our recommendations seem utopian, this may say more about the industry than about our sanity. A writers union simply cannot waver, for instance, on its opposition to indemnification clauses that place potentially ruinous risks on the writer's shoulders and none on the publisher's; the practice is indisputably unjust. Yet because such a clause appears in almost every book contract and an increasing number of magazine contracts, some in the industry will view our position as unwise.

## How to Read the Charts

Where figures are provided, the minima and maxima represent the must-to-avoid and the grail-to-chase. The prevalent range tells you what most people across an entire category, from New York to Podunk, are getting. Of course, we're not telling you to walk away from a decent contract just because you can't negotiate every clause and figure exactly as you'd like it. But we do suggest you consider your experience and clout, then aim as high on that scale as you can.

The Union's role is to aim a little higher still. Our hope is that by providing solid information and promulgating optimistic, fair standards, in the future you won't need quite as much clout to get a fair deal.

# The Periodicals Marketplace

Freelance journalism is an exciting and rewarding professional pursuit. You can choose the subjects you want to write about, interview interesting people, travel, and see your work in print in a matter of weeks or months—sometimes even days.

Freelance journalism can also be a frustrating and defeating cycle of killed stories, late payments, squabbling over expenses, and fighting for the integrity of your stories.

It is a rough world out there, and no journalist alive, no matter how talented and lucky, can claim to have reaped the rewards of the trade without having had to grapple with some of the confusing, undisciplined, and at times outright exploitative practices of the business.

There is no foolproof way to practice safe journalism, but there are things you can do to protect yourself. Learn where the pitfalls are—the more you know about how the business works, the better able you will be to look after your own interests. Sharpen your business skills—by getting better at interpreting contracts, negotiating fees and terms, and collecting payments you prepare yourself to anticipate problems and to deal with them when they do arise.

In this chapter, we will look at the most common problems that confront freelance journalists and suggest ways to address them.

## Queries

The freelance journalism marketplace is vast. There are thousands and thousands of publications that hire freelancers—by some estimates more than 11,000 magazines were published in the United States in 1993. These publications range from national general-interest glossies to special-interest and regional magazines to neighborhood newspapers.

The sheer size of the market is a boon for freelance journalists. But the flip side of the market's size is its growing fragmentation. Publications tend to focus more and more narrowly on precisely defined groups of readers, with editorial content dictated by demographics and advertisers. As a result, freelancers have to deal with larger numbers of publications and need to develop more sophisticated marketing strategies for their story ideas.

In this complex and competitive environment, queries are the lifeblood of a journalist. To make a living from writing, you have to generate a constant stream of ideas and pitch them effectively to publications that are likely to buy them. Query development is a three-part task: You come up with a good concept for an article, identify publications whose audience and editorial focus would be appropriate for the story, and then approach the publications with specifically targeted proposals.

Say you want to do a story on the use of steroids in pigeon racing. You have found a source in the racing community and feel that you can get a real scoop. Where do you take the idea?

You go to the library and look up 'pigeon' in *The Standard Periodical Directory* (Oxbridge Communications Inc., New York, NY). There are several publications dealing with pigeons, among them *American Racing Pigeon News*. Bingo! You have found a perfect market for your story. The story, you feel, might have a broader appeal, however. And you decide to pitch it to *Parade*, *Inside Sports*, and *American Birds*, as well.

Clearly, you need to customize your proposal for each publication. For *American Racing Pigeon News*, an in-depth look at the practice of drugging birds and its impact on the sport would be appropriate. For *Parade*, you may want to propose an exposé about celebrities involved in pigeon "pumping." *Inside Sports* may be interested in a story about corporate sponsorship of pigeon racing, and *American Birds* might buy an article about the effects of steroids on the pigeons themselves.

You get the idea: To market your stories effectively, you have to be knowledgeable about the marketplace and adept at meeting the editorial needs of the publications for which you write.

# Assignments

Imagine. It is early Monday morning. You have dragged yourself out of bed and are trying to focus on the day's headlines while waiting anxiously for the coffee machine to pour the first cup. The phone rings. You give a start and rush to the phone, convinced that the IRS is calling to announce an audit.

To your surprise and jubilation, it is the editor from *Forbes* to whom you recently sent a proposal for a feature story on the new entrepreneurs of the Russian Far East. She wants the story. You discuss the fee, expenses, deadline, and "shake" on the deal.

Ecstatic, you charge the ticket to Vladivostok and begin packing. Here we interrupt the daydream.

An assignment is a business deal, and entering a deal without a written contract is asking for trouble. An assignment is not finalized until you and your editor have agreed to mutually acceptable terms and have signed a contract that clearly spells out those terms.

Although at one time verbal contracts were the norm in the business, most publications now have their own "standard" written contracts for freelance writers. If you get an assignment from one that does not have a standard contract, you should send the editor a letter of agreement outlining all the agreed-upon terms.

It does not really matter where the contract originates. **It is essential, however, that you do not invest significant amounts of time or incur expenses before the deal is finalized with a contract.**

Some will say: "What if the deadline is really tight; how can I wait for a contract?" In fact, some underhanded editors have been known to use this logic to avoid giving writers contracts. The answer is simple: FAX. Today, you can complete negotiations and exchange signed contracts in minutes—provided both parties are willing.

**WARNING!**

# Contracts

Getting an assignment is a thrill. You feel desired, accomplished, and not a little high. It is very important, though, not to let yourself get so lost in the euphoria of the moment that you neglect to negotiate a good deal. The time of assignment is when you have the most leverage.

*All the NWU's recommendations for a good contract are written into its own Standard Journalism Contract. See page 59.*

*More detailed
"Electronic
Rights
Guidelines for
Journalists" are
available to
NWU members.*

*See page 196.*

**NWU**
RECOMMENDS

**For the basic
fee, sell only
one-time
North American
print rights**

The editor is also excited about the story and is likely to be willing to meet at least some of your conditions.

We will now take a look at what constitutes a good deal by examining the various elements that go into a written contract between a freelance journalist and a periodical.

## RIGHTS

Traditionally, periodicals have bought first North American serial rights only. This allowed them to publish the article once in the United States and Canada. To resell or reprint the piece, they had to get the writer's permission and negotiate a separate fee.

In recent years, however, it has become common for periodicals to attempt to seize a variety of other rights—such as syndication, anthology, foreign reprint, and electronic publications—for no extra fee. A typical rights clause in a magazine contract often reads something like this: *Author hereby grants the magazine exclusive worldwide, periodical publication and syndication rights in the article in all languages, in all media including electronic publication, until 120 days after the end of the on-sale period of the issue in which the article appears.* After your eyes unglaze, you will realize that by signing a contract such as this you essentially give away all your rights to the article. Some periodicals go as far as to have journalists sign work-for-hire agreements that strip writers of the copyright to their work.

It is fundamentally unfair for magazines to demand anything other than one-time publication rights. It undermines writers' earning potential, and it makes no economic sense. After all, when you buy a magazine, you do not purchase the right to sell photocopies of the issue. There is a simple principle at play here: One fee, one use.

For the basic fee, negotiate to sell one-time North American print publication rights only. Amend to your contract a phrase like, "All other rights to be negotiated separately."

## RATES

There seems to be no logic to how periodicals pay. There are some small publications that pay as well as national glossies and established magazines that pay as little as regional startups. How do you compare one magazine to another?

The National Union of Journalists in England uses per-page advertising rates to estimate what a periodical's rate structure should be. This is a logical and reliable method. We will be using it in this guide and recommend it as the best way to evaluate magazine pay rates. The rate a page of advertising commands in a particular publication reflects the publication's success and therefore its ability to pay writers. For example, *National Geographic* charges approximately $149,000 for a four-color ad page, and *Time* charges a little over $147,000. Clearly, both publications are in the same, high "success" bracket and should pay writers on the same, high scale.

As you probably know all too well, things do not work this way at present. Even individual publications often do not pay consistent, fair rates to journalists. A lot of intangibles—such as your relationship with the editor, the size of the periodical's inventory, and the day of the week—go into the determination of the rate a publication offers you. But, as radical as this may sound, you have a say in how much you get paid.

Under no circumstances should you accept the editor's first offer without negotiating. Always ask for more money. You will be surprised how often you will succeed.

## KILL FEES

There is only one legitimate reason for a publication not to pay a writer the full fee for an assigned article: the writer's failure to deliver on the terms of the agreement. Unfortunately, more often than not, the kill fee is used as a means to shift most of the financial risk involved in producing a story to the writer.

Circumstances certainly do arise sometimes that make it necessary to kill articles. A news event might make the topic obsolete; a story on the same subject may appear in a rival publication; or the writer and the editor may simply not agree on the angle for the piece. But isn't it profoundly unfair that we, self-supporting writers, should bear the brunt of these uncertainties?

A typical "guarantee" clause in a magazine contract reads something like: "In the event the work is not acceptable and cannot be

*For a fuller explanation of how to use this system, as well as examples of publications within each ad-rate range and the NWU's recommendations for freelance fees, see "Journalism Rates & Practices," page 39.*

J O U R N A L I S M

**NWU RECOMMENDS**

**Always ask for more money**

revised to the publication's satisfaction, the publication will pay the author 25 percent of the agreed-upon fee." Such broad language gives periodicals complete discretion to kill stories. An article can be labeled unacceptable for a great variety of reasons. In fact, many publications now assign more articles than they can use, expecting to kill as many as two of every three.

Editors have to take more responsibility—and assume more of the risk—for selecting writers and assigning articles. The editor, after all, has a kind of final power: if a writer fails to deliver, the editor can choose not to work with that writer again. But if you have done the work, you should get paid. We can again reverse the situation to see how absurd it is. If you buy a magazine and think it is badly written and designed, can you get your money back?

*The NWU says: Kill the kill fee*

It may take a while for kill fees to be abolished, of course. In the meantime, it is essential that contracts spell out as precisely as possible the conditions under which the story can be killed and the amount of the kill fee, which should never be less than one-fourth to one-half of the original fee.

## PAYMENT SCHEDULE

As important as how much you get paid is when you get paid. Your contract may promise you $3,000 for a 1,500-word story, but that will not do you much good if it takes forever to collect. You know how insistent landlords are about getting their rent in actual currency and on time.

Most periodicals contract to pay either on acceptance or on publication. Neither of these choices is advantageous to writers. Many publications carry very large inventories and therefore take months and months to review and accept articles that are submitted on deadline. It takes even longer for stories to get printed. In fact, some articles that are accepted are never published.

To make matters worse, you might have to wait up to several months after the agreed-upon payment time. In the NWU survey, we found that it is common for periodicals to pay 60, 90, or even 120 days after acceptance or publication.

**The best deal is one that provides for payment in full within 30 days of *submission*.** It is your right to be paid as soon as you have rendered your service and not after the publication makes use of the product you delivered. Either that, or we should be able to pay for magazines and newspapers only after we read them. Payment on acceptance is second best; **pay on publication is unacceptable.**

In addition to trying to negotiate better contract terms, you have to be firm and businesslike about collecting payments. Always enclose an invoice when you submit your article. And do not be ashamed of reminding your editor about pending payments. You are not begging, simply running your business.

## EXPENSES

The fee a periodical pays you for an article is meant only to compensate you for your work in researching and writing the story. Since it is often necessary to travel, make long-distance phone calls, and incur other out-of-pocket expenses to get a story, it is a widely accepted practice for publications to reimburse writers for such expenses.

Your contracts with periodicals should always include an "expenses" clause. This clause should detail the types of expenses that will be reimbursed and set a schedule for reimbursement. You will obviously have to supply receipts for the expenses, so a reasonable reimbursement schedule is 15 days after submission of receipts.

## EDITORIAL CONTROL

Few things are quite as deflating and infuriating as to read a just-published article only to realize that a glaring factual error had been introduced during editing. Unfortunately, this happens fairly frequently when writers are not given an opportunity to review the edited version of a story.

Since it is your reputation and credibility that ride on every byline, **insist on seeing proofs of all your stories.** A clause in the contract to that effect is a good way to protect yourself.

It is a good idea to take the "editorial control" clause one step further by reserving the right to remove your byline from the article—without losing the fee—if a dispute about the final form of the article cannot be resolved. In the event that you and your editor simply do not agree on what the story should look like, you will have a legal way to disassociate yourself from the piece and still get paid.

## REVISIONS

As much as we writers may hate the idea, it is reasonable to expect that just about all stories need some rewriting. It is far from reasonable, however, to expect a writer to continue working on the same piece for months—for the same fee.

A good deal will specify the number of revisions covered by the basic fee. One or two revisions is the norm. The contract should also specify that fees for additional revisions will be negotiated based on their extent.

There is no way to avoid rewriting, but you can prevent major disasters by making sure that you and your editor are very clear about the assignment. A detailed description of the assignment should also be included in the contract.

## ARBITRATION

Disputes can arise even if one does everything "right." In a fight, the writer is at a distinct disadvantage. Periodicals tend to be owned by corporations that maintain large legal departments. Few writers, on the other hand, have the money needed for a legal battle.

Arbitration is an inexpensive way to settle disputes, one that is within writers' financial reach. Organizations such as the American Arbitration Association offer arbitration services, which amount to objective hearings and binding decisions. An "arbitration" clause should specify that the arbiter's fee will be shared by the publication and the writer.

## A FINAL WORD ABOUT CONTRACTS

Except for the NWU's Standard Journalism Contract, contracts between writers and publishers usually originate with the publisher. It is vital that you remember two things about magazine publishers' contracts: (1) They are written by the publication's lawyers, who have their client's—not your—interests in mind. (2) You should view them as starting points for negotiations, not as tablets from the mountain.

No matter how much your editor tries to convince you that the contract you got is the periodical's "standard" contract, there is always room for changes. Negotiate. Cross out offensive language. Write in your own conditions. Do whatever it takes to make the assignment a good deal for you.

## PUBLICATION

All right. You struggled to get your foot in the door at the hot new pop-culture magazine, *Seventies Now.* Your proposal for "Tie-dye in the 90s" got a lot of interest, and you got the assignment. You negotiated hard, got a good fee, and a solid contract. The story turned out well. You got paid (on submission). And then you waited . . . and waited.

Many periodicals maintain huge inventories; so articles sometimes do not appear until months after deadline. Our survey showed that a delay of 8 to 12 weeks between submission and publication is common. For a monthly, that is "timely." But way-longer delays are not extraordinary.

Unfortunately, there is little a writer can do to protect against getting lost in inventory. You cannot write a publication date into the contract. At most, you can choose not to work for publications where you have gotten burned. And if enough of us do that, we might just create an industry standard for timely publication.

# *Journalism Rates & Practices*

Freelance journalists write for thousands of different publications, from national glossies and regional magazines to trade and professional publications to newspapers of all sizes and circulations. It is obviously impossible to generalize about such a broad range of markets. Therefore, to make our discussion of rates and practices in journalism sensible, we present information for four groups of publication for which freelance journalists write: consumer magazines, trade magazines, professional magazines, and newspapers.

## *Rates*

How do you know what is a reasonable pay rate to expect from a magazine?

In this guide, we use the system employed by the National Union of Journalists in England, in which pay rates are established commensurate with publications' advertising rates. This is an equitable and logical system, since it links a magazine's financial relationship with freelance writers to its economic prosperity.

Since most of us are not used to thinking of the rates we get from magazines as a function of what they charge for advertising, figuring out an acceptable rate for a specific magazine might take a little getting used to. But the system is easy to use.

### STEP 1.

### Find out the publication's rate for a full-page, four-color ad.

We subdivided three types of periodicals—consumer magazines, trade publications, and professional publications—into categories based on the cost of one page of advertising. (Since newspaper ad-rate structures are more complex, we have subdivided them according to geographic scope.) If it is not one of those listed in the Guide, you can also get this information from the Standard Rate & Data Service directories, which are available at many libraries, or from the magazine's media kit, which anyone can get by calling the publisher's advertising department.

### STEP 2.

**Compare the magazine to others in its ad-rate group to decide what kind of rate to negotiate for.**

In each subcategory, we provide a list of examples of publications that charge those rates. Then we give you the range of rates paid to freelance writers in that category, along with the NWU's recommended freelance rates for the category.

For instance, if you are interested in *Parenting*, which charges $37,925 per page of advertising and, therefore, belongs in Group 6, you would likely try to get $1.50–$2.00 a word. On the other hand, if you were interested in *Good Housekeeping*, which is also in Group 6, but charges $21,200 for a page of advertising, you would probably negotiate for a rate in the $1–$1.50 range.

**Before talking about money,** arm yourself with as much information as you can. Ask the editor what they pay for various sections of the magazine, but also talk to other writers who have written there.

### STEP 3.

**Consider all your needs and options before negotiating.**

There are always individual considerations in valuing one's work. You may really want the exposure of a national publication, for instance, and therefore accept a lower fee from an adamant editor. Or you may need to pay for next month's groceries, and so decide not to hold out for an extra 10 cents a word.

But always estimate carefully how long a piece will take to write; including editing and fact-checking time. Figure out how much you need to make for that period, and if you cannot get paid a living wage, reconsider.

**WARNING!**

**Remember that magazine publishing is a business. No commercial enterprise needs you to subsidize it, and unless you have somebody subsidizing you, you can't afford to do so.**

(The recommendations are for magazines where you work to earn money. If you are writing for a publication that supports a particular cause that you want to contribute to, you may want to accept a reduced fee, or do the work *pro bono*.)

You might think it is unrealistic and self-defeating to ask for $2 a word if you are used to getting half that or less. But the fact is that freelance journalists are grossly underpaid, and it is up to us to begin to change the situation.

The recommendations we make here are meant to start an incremental change in the industry. There is a wide gap between current economic conditions in the freelance journalism market and the equitable conditions that should exist. The **minimum standards** we propose here represent the first step in bridging this gap.

J
O
U
R
N
A
L
I
S
M

## PAY RATES

### CONSUMER MAGAZINES

We subdivided the consumer magazine market into seven ad-rate groups, based on the cost of a full-page, four-color ad.[1] Below is a list of the groups, along with examples of magazines that fall within them.

| | |
|---|---|
| **Group 1**<br>**$200,000 and over** | Modern Maturity, Parade |
| **Group 2**<br>**$100,000–$200,000** | Family Circle, National Geographic, Newsweek, People, Reader's Digest, Sports Illustrated, Time, TV Guide, Woman's Day |
| **Group 3**<br>**$80,000–$100,000** | Car & Driver, McCall's, Money, Playboy, Redbook, US News & World Report |
| **Group 4**<br>**$60,000–$80,000** | American Baby, Business Week, Cosmopolitan, Field & Stream, Glamour, Golf Digest, Poolife, Popular Mechanics |
| **Group 5**<br>**$40,000–$60,000** | Automobile, Child, Conde Nast Traveler, Country Home, Elle, Esquire, Forbes, Harper's Bazaar, Men's Health, New York Times Magazine, PC, Seventeen, The New Yorker, US, Vanity Fair, Vogue |
| **Group 6**<br>**$20,000–$40,000** | Allure, Atlantic Monthly, Boating, Chicago Tribune Magazine, Details, Ebony, Good Housekeeping, Mature Outlook, Modern Bride, Muscle & Fitness, New York, Parenting, Penthouse, Premier, Prevention, Pulse, Town & Country, Victoria |
| **Group 7**<br>**$20,000 and under** | Advocate, American Way, Art & Antique, Black Enterprise, Buzz, Cat Fancy, CD Rom World, Cigar Aficionado, Entertainment Weekly, Fitness, Hispanic, Interview, Longevity, Mother Jones, Pacific Northwest, Playgirl, Vermont Magazine |

[1]Source: Standard Rate & Data Service

| (IN $ PER WORD) | | | ★ NWU Recommends (at least) | |
|---|---|---|---|---|
| Low | Prevalent Range | High | | |
| $0.67 | $1.00—$2.00 | $3.00 | $1.25—$2.50 | **Group 1** **$200,000 and over** |
| $0.40 | $1.00—$2.00 | $3.00 | $1.25—$2.50 | **Group 2** **$100,000—$200,000** |
| $0.33 | $1.00—$2.00 | $2.50 | $1.25—$2.50 | **Group 3** **$80,000—$100,000** |
| $0.33 | $1.00—$1.75 | $2.00 | $1.25—$2.20 | **Group 4** **$60,000—$80,000** |
| $0.33 | $0.75—$1.50 | $2.00 | $1.00—$2.00 | **Group 5** **$40,000—$60,000** |
| $0.33 | $0.75—$1.50 | $2.00 | $1.00—$2.00 | **Group 6** **$20,000—$40,000** |
| $0.25 | $0.50—$1.25 | $1.50 | $0.75—$1.50 | **Group 7** **$20,000 and under** |

## PAY RATES

### TRADE PUBLICATIONS

Pay rates for trade publications can also be linked to the magazines' economic performances as expressed by their advertising rates. Below are the four ad-rate groups into which trade publications are divided.

| | |
|---|---|
| **Group 1**<br>**$20,000 and over** | Byte, Computerworld, Financial World, Industry Week, Realtor News |
| **Group 2**<br>**$10,000–$20,000** | Adweek, Cheers, Chief Executive, Crain's New York Business, Home Office Computing |
| **Group 3**<br>**$5,000–$10,000** | Architecture, American Demographics, Billboard, Publisher's Weekly, Woman Engineer |
| **Group 4**<br>**$5,000 and under** | CPA Today, Decor, Nails, Real Estate Forum, Vermont Business |

### PROFESSIONAL PUBLICATIONS

Pay rates in professional publications can be considered in light of the publications' advertising rates, too. Since many professional publications are printed in two or even one color, we looked at their ad rates for **full-page, black and white advertising**. The groups are as follows:

| | |
|---|---|
| **Group 1**<br>**$10,000 and over** | ABA Journal, Electronic Engineering Times, Defense Electronics |
| **Group 2**<br>**$5,000–$10,000** | American Educator, American Journalism Review, American Lawyer, Computer Design, Medical Economics |
| **Group 3**<br>**$5,000 and under** | Academe, Counseling Today, Family Planning World, Library Journal, Lingua Franca, Museum News, Printed Circuit Design, Trial |

| (IN $ PER WORD) | | | ★ NWU Recommends (at least) | |
| Low | Prevalent Range | High | | |
| --- | --- | --- | --- | --- |
| $0.33 | $0.50—$1.00 | $1.25 | $0.75—$1.25 | Group 1 ($20,000 and over) |
| $0.25 | $0.40—$1.00 | $1.25 | $0.50—$1.25 | Group 2 ($10,000–$20,000) |
| $0.10 | $0.25—$0.75 | $1.00 | $0.30—$1.00 | Group 3 ($5,000–$10,000) |
| $0.10 | $0.25—$0.75 | $1.00 | $0.30—$1.00 | Group 4 ($5,000 and under) |

| $0.33 | $0.50—$1.00 | $1.25 | $0.75—$1.25 | Group 1 ($10,000 and over) |
| --- | --- | --- | --- | --- |
| $0.25 | $0.40—$1.00 | $1.25 | $0.50—$1.25 | Group 2 ($5,000–$10,000) |
| $0.10 | $0.25—$0.75 | $1.00 | $0.30—$1.00 | Group 3 ($5,000 and under) |

## PAY RATES

### NEWSPAPERS

Newspapers, especially those that publish several editions, tend to have more complex advertising-rate structures than magazines. It is, therefore, more difficult to compare newspapers based on this criterion. A more practical way is to group newspapers according to their geographic scope. We identified four groups: national dailies, national weeklies, state/regional, and local.

| | | ($ PER WORD) Prevalent Range | ★ NWU Recommends (at least) |
|---|---|---|---|
| **Group 1 National Dailies** | New York Times, Los Angeles Times, Wall Street Journal, Washington Post | $0.25—$0.90 | $0.30—$1.15 |
| **Group 2 National Weeklies** | LA Weekly, Village Voice, National Employment Weekly, New York Observer | $0.25—$0.80 | $0.30—$1.00 |
| **Group 3 State / Regional** | Boston Globe, Chicago Sun Times, Dallas Morning News, Miami Herald, Newsday, Phoenix Republic Gazette, San Francisco Examiner | $0.10—$0.65 | $0.15—$0.80 |
| **Group 4 Local** | Boston Phoenix, Buffalo News, New York Post, San Diego Union Examiner, Tallahassean | $0.05—$0.35 | $0.10—$0.50 |

# *Practices*

The treatment writers receive from the publications we work for is just as important as how much we get paid. Such issues as kill fees, rights, and contracts are of universal concern. In these matters, however, there is no need to differentiate among publications. A local newspaper should treat freelance journalists as well as a glossy national magazine. That is why the National Writers Union is calling for consistent minimum standards of industry practice.

## CONTRACTS

Freelance writing is a business, and every story assignment is a business deal that should be concluded with a written contract. Many writers, however, seem to discount the importance of contracts. In our research, we found the following trend.

| CONTRACT USE | | |
|---|---|---|
| *Freelance journalists writing for* | Use contracts | Do not use contracts |
| **Consumer magazines** | 53.5% | 46.5% |
| **Trade publications** | 39% | 61% |
| **Professional publications** | 43% | 57% |
| **Newspapers** | 34% | 66% |

The responsibility for such behavior lies equally with publishers, of course. Editors will often give the excuse that there is no time to deal with a contract, especially if the assignment involves a time-sensitive subject. A fax machine, of course, quickly takes care of this obstacle to signing a written agreement.

But ultimately, we writers are accountable for our own businesses. If you sell a story to a magazine that does not use contracts, outline the agreement in a letter, sign it, and send it to the editor. This is a common practice in cases where assignments are made verbally, and it is highly advisable.

J
O
U
R
N
A
L
I
S
M

Many writers do not even protect themselves in this simple way, however. Here is what we found when we asked freelance journalists about their use of confirmation letters.

| USE OF CONFIRMATION LETTERS (for assignments given verbally) | | |
| --- | --- | --- |
| Freelance journalists writing for | Use | Do not use |
| **Consumer magazines** | 31% | 69% |
| **Trade publications** | 28% | 72% |
| **Professional publications** | 37% | 63% |
| **Newspapers** | 24% | 76% |

"I've known my editor for years," many writers say. "I don't need written agreements or contracts." It is true that publishing traditionally operated on handshakes, secured by the personal relationships between writers and editors. But publishing is not what it used to be; the editor with whom you establish a relationship today is quite likely to be gone tomorrow. In any case, you are not entering an agreement with the editor but with the very large corporation for which the editor probably works.

**Always protect yourself with a written contract or confirmation letter.**

NWU
RECOMMENDS

## RIGHTS

Until fairly recently, publishers of periodicals were content to buy first North American serial rights only—i.e., the right to publish an article once in the United States and Canada. If they wanted to reprint or resell the story, they had to get the writer's permission and negotiate a separate fee.

Periodicals are now frequently attempting to seize many other rights—such as syndication, anthology, foreign reprint, and electronic—for no extra fee. Some publications actually go as far as to have journalists sign work-for-hire agreements, in which the writer assigns the copyright for a piece to the publication.

*See page 11 for more details on work-for-hire contracts.*

To find out the extent of the problem, we asked freelance journalists whether publications for which they wrote in the preceding 12 months requested rights other than first North American print rights.

---

**PUBLICATIONS ASK FOR MORE THAN FIRST NORTH AMERICAN PRINT RIGHTS**

| Freelance journalists writing for | Yes | No |
|---|---|---|
| **Consumer magazines** | 79% | 21% |
| **Trade publications** | 81.5% | 18.5% |
| **Professional publications** | 83% | 17% |
| **Newspapers** | 86% | 14% |

---

We then asked which additional rights publishers generally tried to obtain. The breakdowns are given in the chart below as percentages of those publishers who required writers to sign over additional rights.

---

**ADDITIONAL RIGHTS REQUESTED** (by percentage of publishers)

| | Foreign | Electronic | Syndication | Wire | Anthology |
|---|---|---|---|---|---|
| **Consumer magazines** | 63% | 56% | 66% | 43% | 62% |
| **Trade publications** | 36% | 51% | 40% | 31% | 40.5% |
| **Professional publications** | 40% | 44.5% | 53.5% | 36% | 57% |
| **Newspapers** | 38% | 41.5% | 50% | 35% | 30% |

---

Finally, we wanted to find out how likely freelance journalists are to sign over rights other than first North American print rights. We asked writers whether they complied with publishers' requests for additional rights and found the following.

*For a more complete discussion of electronic rights, see page 21.*

**ADDITIONAL RIGHTS GRANTED** (by percentage of writers)

| Freelance journalists writing for | Signed over additional rights | Did not sign over additional rights |
|---|---|---|
| **Consumer magazines** | 44.5% | 55.5% |
| **Trade publications** | 41% | 59% |
| **Professional publications** | 49% | 51% |
| **Newspapers** | 31% | 69% |

**NWU**
**RECOMMENDS**

Publishers' demands for any rights other than one-time publication rights are fundamentally unfair and economically inequitable. **The National Writers Union has long called for the principle of 'One fee, one use' to be adapted as the industry standard.**

A good deal, like the one outlined in the NWU's Standard Journalism Contract (page 61), is one that is based on the idea of **one fee, one use. For the basic fee, negotiate to sell one-time North American print publication rights only.** Other rights should be sold separately.

## PAYMENTS

**TIMING OF PAYMENTS**

When you get paid is almost as important as how much you get paid. Most publications contract to pay either on acceptance or on publication—terms not favorable to writers. Our research showed the following trend.

| | On submission | On acceptance | On publication |
|---|---|---|---|
| **Consumer magazines** | 10.5% | 55.2% | 34.3% |
| **Trade publications** | 14.8% | 41.1% | 44.1% |
| **Professional publications** | 14.1% | 47.3% | 38.6% |
| **Newspapers** | 11% | 34.6% | 54.4% |
| **NWU Recommends** | **Full payment on submission** | | |

Payment on submission precludes the use of kill fees—one of the most insidious practices in the industry. (See "Kill Fees" below.)

*For discussion of pay schedules, see page 34.*

---

**PAYMENT DELAYS**

It is unfair enough that publishers force writers to wait for payment until they deem our work acceptable. To make matters worse, you might have to wait up to several months after the agreed-upon payment time. In the NWU survey, we found the following pattern of delays in payment.

|  | Prevalent range | NWU recommends (no later than) |
|---|---|---|
|  | (weeks after agreed-upon payment time) | |
| **Consumer magazines** | 2—8 | I week |
| **Trade publications** | 2—6 | I week |
| **Professional publications** | 2—8 | I week |
| **Newspapers** | 2—12 | I week |

---

To protect yourself, get a payment date from the publication and hold them to it.

Payment on acceptance is okay—and, for now, standard practice. However, **the best deal is one that provides for payment in full within 30 days of *submission*.**

## KILL FEES

The kill fee is an insidious device. It allows publishers to decide at the last minute—and at their full discretion—whether to use an assigned article or not. And the only penalty they pay is a small fraction of the contracted-for fee.

Here is what we found about kill fees in our research.

### HOW MANY STORIES CANCELED IN PREVIOUS 12 MONTHS?

|  | None | 1—4 | 5+ |
|---|---|---|---|
| **Consumer magazines** | 84% | 15% | 1% |
| **Trade publications** | 84% | 15% | 1% |
| **Professional publications** | 84% | 14.5% | 1.5% |
| **Newspapers** | 84% | 15% | 1% |

### RECEIVED KILL FEES FOR CANCELED STORIES?

|  | Yes | No |
|---|---|---|
| **Consumer magazines** | 51% | 49% |
| **Trade publications** | 44% | 56% |
| **Professional publications** | 58% | 42% |
| **Newspapers** | 45% | 55% |

### KILL FEE AS PERCENTAGE OF CONTRACTED FEE

|  | 0—25% | 26—50% | 51—100% |
|---|---|---|---|
| **Consumer magazines** | 41.3% | 29.3% | 29.4% |
| **Trade publications** | 48.3% | 25.9% | 25.8% |
| **Professional publications** | 17.3% | 47.7% | 35% |
| **Newspapers** | 35.7% | 38% | 26.3% |

NWU
RECOMMENDS

The National Writers Union holds that a writer who fulfills the terms of his or her contract should be paid in full, regardless of whether the publisher decides to print the article.

It is obviously going to be difficult to convince publishers to stop using kill fees all at once. **If you cannot get kill fees out of your contracts, we recommend that you negotiate them up as high as possible.**

## EXPENSES

It is often necessary to spend money on travel, phone calls, research fees, and so on. If writers were to pay these expenses out of the fees paid by magazines, we would have little to show for our labors. Unfortunately, a great many freelance journalists do subsidize publishers by paying the expenses they incur in researching and writing stories.

**NWU RECOMMENDS**

**HOW OFTEN ARE EXPENSES REIMBURSED BY PUBLISHERS?**

|  | Always | Sometimes | Never |
|---|---|---|---|
| **Consumer magazines** | 56.6% | 12.6% | 30.8% |
| **Trade publications** | 53.9% | 15.6% | 30.5% |
| **Professional publications** | 58.5% | 8.2% | 33.3% |
| **Newspapers** | 43.9% | 15% | 41.1% |

**All reasonable expenses must be reimbursed by the magazine within 15 days of submission of receipts.**

Make sure your contracts include a clause that specifies what will be considered reasonable expenses and the maximum amount the publication agrees to reimburse. If you are going to exceed the agreed-upon maximum, call up the editor and follow up with a confirmation letter.

**NWU RECOMMENDS**

## REVISIONS

Contracts should specify the number of rewrites included in the fee, and additional revisions have to be paid for separately. Currently, this is rarely the case.

### HOW MANY REWRITES, ON AVERAGE, WERE REQUIRED FOR ARTICLES PUBLISHED IN THE LAST 12 MONTHS?

| | None | 1 | 2 | 3+ |
|---|---|---|---|---|
| **Consumer magazines** | 62% | 27.3% | 6.7% | 3% |
| **Trade publications** | 71.6% | 22% | 3.4% | 2% |
| **Professional publications** | 56.1% | 34.2% | 7% | 2.7% |
| **Newspapers** | 69.8% | 21% | 6.3% | 2.9% |

### HOW MANY REWRITES WERE SPECIFIED BY THE CONTRACT, IF ANY?

| | None | 1+ |
|---|---|---|
| **Consumer magazines** | 73.2% | 26.8% |
| **Trade publications** | 77.8% | 22.2% |
| **Professional publications** | 62.5% | 37.5% |
| **Newspapers** | 78% | 22% |

### WERE ADDITIONAL REWRITES PAID FOR?

| | Yes | No |
|---|---|---|
| **Consumer magazines** | 3.2% | 96.8% |
| **Trade publications** | 5% | 95% |
| **Professional publications** | 5.8% | 94.2% |
| **Newspapers** | 4.3% | 95.7% |

NWU
RECOMMENDS

Contracts should specify that one (1) revision of the article will be provided by the writer and that a separate fee will be paid for additional rewrites.

## Editorial Control

Freelancers often complain that their stories are changed without permission. We wanted to find out how prevalent this practice is. Here is what freelance journalists told us in response to our asking whether any of the stories they had written in the previous 12 months had been altered without their approval.

| STORIES ALTERED WITHOUT WRITER'S APPROVAL | | |
|---|---|---|
| | Yes | No |
| **Consumer magazines** | 25.8% | 74.2% |
| **Trade publications** | 25.3% | 74.7% |
| **Professional publications** | 24.1% | 75.9% |
| **Newspapers** | 22.8% | 77.2% |

Writers have every right to see the final, edited versions of their stories before publication. After all, our names and reputations, to say nothing of professional pride, ride on every article.

**Journalism contracts should include an "editorial control" clause that ensures that the writer will have the opportunity to review and make changes to the final, edited version of the article.**

NWU
Recommends

## Publication

The National Writers Union holds that timely publication is important for writers and calls on the industry as a whole to strive for the establishment of reasonable standards.

## MULTIPLE SUBMISSIONS

We asked writers whether they submitted queries or proposals for stories to more than one publication simultaneously.

| USE SIMULTANEOUS SUBMISSION | | |
|---|---|---|
| | Yes | No |
| **Consumer magazines** | 20% | 80% |
| **Trade publications** | 18% | 82% |
| **Professional publications** | 21% | 79% |
| **Newspapers** | 23% | 77% |

Although the NWU does not recommend that you always submit queries to more than one publication at a time, such simultaneous submissions can improve your chances of selling a story in a shorter time.

## RESPONSE TO QUERIES

Another concern that freelance journalists raise is the amount of time it takes publications to respond to queries. In our research we found the following patterns.

| QUERY RESPONSE TIME | |
|---|---|
| | Average (in weeks) |
| **Consumer magazines** | 4.2 |
| **Trade publications** | 2.4 |
| **Professional publications** | 3.6 |
| **Newspapers** | 1.5 |

## WRITING ON SPEC

Writing on spec—i.e., doing the research and writing on your own time and then trying to sell the finished story—is one of those issues about which people tend to have very strong feelings. Some swear by it; others think it is preposterous.

| **WRITING ON SPEC** | | |
|---|---|---|
| *Freelance journalists writing for* | Yes | No |
| **Consumer magazines** | 26% | 84% |
| **Trade publications** | 27% | 83% |
| **Professional publications** | 21.4% | 79.6% |
| **Newspapers** | 22.5% | 77.5% |

**Don't write on spec. Submit queries rather than completed articles. It is difficult enough to make a living as a freelance journalist without assuming the financial risk of working on spec.**

NWU
RECOMMENDS

Some people might respond to everything we have talked about in this chapter by saying that it is easy for the NWU to talk about setting standards, but that it is the individual writer who has the tough job of negotiating fees and contracts. In one sense that is true: as freelancers we all have to take responsibility for our own businesses. But the NWU also provides information, education, support, and grievance assistance. We have the Standard Journalism Contract and provide writers with training in using it.

*More on the Standard Journalism Contract: page 59.*

If enough of us stand up for our rights, to paraphrase Arlo Guthrie's "Alice's Restaurant," they (publishers) might think it's a movement. And it is.

# The NWU Standard Journalism Contract

BY JUDITH LEVINE

Twenty-five or 30 years ago, there was no such thing as a kill fee. Every publication bought only one-time rights, and—most shocking of all—a person could support a family as a full-time magazine writer.

Since then, rates have not increased; in real dollars, they've shrunk. As the Guide makes clear, conditions and contracts are ever more unfavorable to writers.

How can we improve working conditions, shift the balance of power between publishers and writers, and raise professional standards for every freelancer in the periodicals industry—starting now?

The answer is the National Writers Union Standard Journalism Contract (SJC). Not a traditional "collective-bargaining" agreement where the union signs a contract with a publication covering all the freelancers who work for it, the SJC can be used by any Writers Union member at any magazine she writes for. She presents it at the moment of her greatest power—when the magazine has decided it wants this article from her. And while she is using it, other writers at many other publications—and at the same publication—are using it too. Like the NWU, a united body of far-flung workers laboring in isolation, the SJC is a collective effort carried out by individuals, backed by the power of numbers.

## What's in It?

The contract lays out what every writer wants: an even deal. Under its terms, the writer agrees to do the job competently, originally, and on time, and to provide one revision. In return, the publisher pays promptly and in full, buys one-time print rights only, defends the writer in libel suits, and shares the cost of arbitration should a dispute arise.

There is no kill fee in the SJC. This forces editors to assign judiciously and sharpen vague ideas at the beginning of the process, before it's too late. Stories for which there is little commitment at the magazine may go unassigned. The results: better working relationships and better stories.

Although a writer may not always succeed in getting the union contract signed, the very act of introducing and discussing it with editors changes the language of the industry and alters the writer's position in it. By serving as a model of fair and respectful conduct and a benchmark against which to measure other contracts, the SJC helps writers improve the terms of publishers' contracts, too—achieving better terms every time they negotiate an assignment.

For many writers, saying "I am a National Writers Union member, and I use our Standard Contract" is a strange, scary, and exhilarating experience. Sending the SJC—a document that doesn't mention a kill fee and sells only one use for one fee—feels audacious, and frankly, utopian. Yet putting a contract in the mail to a client is normal practice for professionals and artisans in every other freelance business, from management consulting to linoleum installing.

*Sending out the Standard Journalism Contract feels audacious, even utopian*

## Good for the Industry

The union contract is a benefit of membership, and its use is part of a wider campaign to expand writers' rights in a marketplace that considers these less and less. At contract orientation sessions, writers share information about editors, fees, publishers' contracts, and developments in the industry. They practice negotiating skills tailored to the union contract, but flexible enough for any contract. The union's experienced Journalism Campaign leaders and grievance officers are available to help members decipher, negotiate, and amend contracts, and resolve problems if they occur.

The NWU contract is good not only for writers, but also for magazine publishing as a whole. Contracts that starve writers of rights,

STANDARD JOURNALISM CONTRACT

UAW/AFL-CIO

Contract between (Writer) _____

and (Publisher) _____

1. The Writer agrees to prepare an Article of _____ words on the subject of:

_____

_____

_____

for delivery on or before _____ (date). The Writer also agrees to provide one revision of the Article.

2. The Publisher agrees to pay the Writer a fee of $_____within thirty (30) days of initial receipt of the Article as assigned above. (In other words, an original and coherent manuscript of approximately the above word count on the subject assigned, and for which appropriate research was completed.)

3. The Publisher agrees that the above fee purchases one-time North American hard-copy print publication rights only. All other rights, including the electronic reproduction, transmission, display, performance or distribution of the Article, are fully reserved by the Writer.

4. The Publisher agrees to reimburse the Writer for all previously agreed-upon and documented expenses within fifteen (15) days of submission of receipts.

5. The Publisher agrees to make every reasonable effort to make available to the Writer, the final, edited version of the Article while there is still time to make changes. In the event of a disagreement over the final form of the Article, the Writer reserves the right to withdraw his/her name from the Article without prejudicing the agreed-upon fee.

6. The Writer guarantees that the Article will not contain material that is consciously libelous or defamatory. In return, the Publisher agrees to provide and pay for counsel to defend the Writer in any litigation arising as a result of the Article.

7. In the event of a dispute between the Writer and the Publisher that cannot be resolved through the National Writers Union (NWU) grievance process, the Writer will have the option of seeking to resolve the matter by arbitration, or in court. If arbitration is chosen, the Writer may be represented by the NWU in any procedures before the arbitrator. The arbitrator's fees shall be shared fifty percent (50%) by the Publisher and fifty percent (50%) by the Writer. Any decision reached by the arbitrator may be appealed pursuant to applicable law.

_____        _____
Writer or Writer's Representative        Publisher's Representative

_____        _____
Date:                                                Date:

legal protection, and decent fees are the death certificates of the periodicals industry, for good writers will no longer be willing or able to write for magazines. The SJC is an important step toward improving writers' declining economic lot and gaining them a measure of equality in dealing with publishers. By establishing rules and standards where none exist, it helps restore fairness, professionalism, and civility to the periodicals industry.

# Freelancing from Afar

BY DAVID LIDA

As a youth, I had two compelling fantasies: making a living as a writer and living in a foreign country. I began to realize the first in 1983, when I got a job at a newspaper, *Women's Wear Daily*. Seven years later, the second fantasy crystallized. My goal was no longer "a foreign country," but Mexico City, a place that had enchanted me during numerous visits.

I was 30. I had freelanced full-time for two-and-a-half years (after five on staff at *WWD*), thus building enough contacts in the magazine world to give me the confidence to make the move.

Professionally, I was as methodical as possible before leaving. I spent days in the library, researching every story angle that might interest any imaginable publication. I met with editors I knew and contacted others I didn't. These efforts resulted in a few assignments and the promise of more later.

Nonetheless, not long after I arrived in Mexico, I experienced the freelancer's familiar panic attack. In one day, I was hit with a one-two punch. An editor at *Connoisseur*, who gave me an assignment before I left, called to say the magazine had been taken over by a new editorial team, which no longer wanted the story. Another magazine, *Diversion*, which had encouraged me on two ideas, decided they wanted only one and offered so little money that it wasn't worth the effort.

Before moving I had bought a fax machine and was optimistic about long-distance communication with editors via this (for me) new technology. However, I soon realized that it was just as easy for them to ignore faxes as it had been to disregard phone calls.

Although as a New York freelance I had been no stranger to insecurity, my sense of doubt was intensified by the lack of proximity to my sources of work. Fresh worries appeared: What if I never get another assignment? What if all the editors forget I exist? Will I be able to work in a taco stand?

However, soon after the one-two punch, I was redeemed by calls from two distinct publications: *Bride's*, which assigned me a honeymoon travel piece about Pacific Coast beaches, and *The Advocate*, which wanted a cover story about AIDS activism in Mexico. These were publications I hadn't even thought of soliciting when I lived in New York.

Their calls inspired me to become more expansive in my search for work. I don't claim to have found a foolproof method of staying alive as a freelance in a foreign country. In fact, survival might require a different strategy in each place we've dreamed of living. However, a mixture of doggedness and imagination helped me to consistently gain assignments in Mexico.

I looked farther and wider—not only editorially but geographically. When Canada was announced as part of the North American Free Trade Agreement, I went to the Canadian embassy in Mexico City and did research on that country's publications. After considering the Mexican population in California, I did similar research about L.A.-based magazines. I made a dozen blind solicitations.

Although an imperfect, almost arbitrary, way to do business, it bore fruit. The Canadian research resulted in an assignment from a supplement to the *Toronto Globe & Mail*, about drawn-out, drunken Mexican business lunches. While the Los Angeles investigation didn't conclude with any jobs, one L.A. editor recommended me for a lucrative story for a Hong Kong airline magazine (about the different ways Spanish is spoken throughout Latin America). Similarly, I sent many of my articles to *Vogue*'s travel editor in New York, and although he never gave me work, he recommended me to two other magazines which did.

The need to make a living also propelled me to spread my wings journalistically. I wrote about nearly every conceivable topic: politics, business, the arts and entertainment, science, architecture, food, bullfighting. The exigencies of the freelance life drove me to learn more about Mexico in two years than I would have if I'd had a regular job or, I suspect, a regular journalist's job at a bureau or wire service.

Survival through lean periods was easier because Mexico City's cost of living is roughly half of New York's. Therefore, I could take on certain assignments whose fees would have been lamentable for a New Yorker, such as $700 for a long profile of a woman bullfighter for *The Village Voice*, or $600 (plus $200 expenses) for a *New York Times* travel-section feature on an archeological site in Veracruz. These paychecks were by no means extravagant, but, my monthly rent, to give an idea, was $330; a taxi from my apartment to the airport cost $7; and dinner out in an elegant restaurant ran about $25 (more modest meals were as little as $2). I have often thought I'd have had a tougher time if, instead of Mexico City, I'd fallen in love with Paris or Tokyo.

The slower pace of life in Mexico, and the fact that accomplishing anything takes more time than Americans are accustomed to, was annoying—but in another sense, beneficial.

Let me explain. Once or twice a week, I would walk to the post office—an errand which took 45 minutes round-trip—because leaving letters in a mailbox is too risky in a country whose postal system is dangerously unreliable. My journey was yet longer when I needed typewriter ribbons. These errands—as well as getting around an impossibly large and confusing city on assignments—were not wasted time. They awakened in me the process of discovery. I got to know the look, texture and subtleties of Mexico City street life, which made my writing about Mexico more vivid.

In the course of these missions, I had a lot of time to think—not only about the articles I was working on, but my experience in my adopted country. When I wasn't working on a story, soliciting new work, or writing dunning letters, I spent a lot of time in cafes and cantinas—sometimes with other writers, sometimes with people who had nothing to do with my profession, sometimes alone.

I can't overly emphasize the importance of those hours of peaceful reflection. Living in Mexico, where most people work to live and not vice versa, helped me learn to live in the present. In contrast, in New York much of our lives are spent planning the future, in fast-paced blips and sound bites, brief encounters and harried phone messages. The constant struggle to survive fosters an ethic wherein moments of meditation make one uneasy. When writers have a free moment in New York, we ask ourselves: Why have I nothing to do? What *should* I be doing? (soliciting another editor, polishing a rewrite?)

I think for many writers it is a dirty secret that we don't sit down and write eight hours a day—that some of our best work is accomplished walking around thinking, reading, or sitting in a cafe having a conversation. In contrast to the self-important atmosphere, breathless pace, and brutal expense of New York, the relative tranquillity of my life in Mexico made me comfortable with that reality.

If the cantinas were cozy, there were also some difficult aspects to working in Mexico. For example, press officers of most government agencies perceive their jobs as sort of town criers: through communiques or press conferences, they disseminate officially sanctioned information. Trying to obtain any other data—even harmless statistics with no controversial significance—can be an ordeal. A story for *Longevity* about pollution in Mexico City—an assignment I thought would be easy, given how much had been written on the subject—turned out to be a bureaucratic nightmare, demanding months of research from primarily hostile sources.

For one line of a story I wrote for *The Advocate*, I needed to confirm an accusation that the state-owned oil company tested all prospective administrative employees for HIV as a condition of employment. The company spokeswoman was nonplused by my query and managed to stall several weeks, claiming that the only person in the entire company who could answer my question was unavailable (a frequent, if ludicrous,

tactic from Mexican bureaucrats). Since I didn't have a pressing deadline, I finally obtained a juicy, damning quote from her. Had I been working for a daily, I would have had to use a variation of "Officials were unavailable for comment."

Even from non-official sources, obtaining information could be a trial. For example, the *hemerotecas* (periodicals libraries) of Mexico City have no card catalogues, computers, or indexes. If you don't know which issue of a particular publication you're seeking, you're damned to look through periodicals day by day, month by month, hoping to unearth the desired information.

Also, the culture of what has been called *mañana-ismo* is still in place. Although the situation has improved somewhat in the past few years, many Mexicans, even gung-ho businessmen, arrive late for appointments and sometimes don't show up at all. This is by no means judged as harshly as it would be in the U.S. Nonetheless, living in Mexico was a wonderful experience for me and my first few months back in New York were very difficult. Although the phones invariably function, the library is computerized, and one o'clock really means one o'clock, New York seemed sterile, cold, and devoid of spontaneity. I missed Mexico terribly.

# Building a Better Book Contract[1]

BY PHILIP MATTERA

Each book contract is a milestone in the life of a writer. Yet the excitement of having a publisher express interest in your work is usually followed by feelings of confusion and disappointment. You are dismayed to find that the contract sent to you for signing contains provisions that are either indecipherable or totally one sided in favor of the publisher.

The National Writers Union believes that authors need not be powerless or uninformed when it comes to book contracts—whether or not you are represented by an agent. Book contracts are complicated documents that often reflect entrenched industry practices favoring publishers, but they are not beyond comprehension. This chapter is meant to give authors a basic orientation to contract issues, which are analyzed in much greater depth in the *NWU Guide to Book Contracts*.

When considering an offer from a publisher, keep in mind that proposed contracts are not take-it-or-leave-it propositions; you should never simply sign on the dotted line. Certain provisions may have been agreed on orally by you or your agent and have to be regarded as given, but everything else in the contract should be considered up for grabs—though to varying degrees. Some provisions in the publisher's standard contract (known as boilerplate) are easy to change, some

*Boilerplate contracts are not take-it-or-leave it propositions. Don't just sign on the dotted line*

can be changed with difficulty, and some can only be changed if you are a "big name" or someone with a hot project. (The commercial book business is not egalitarian.) Still other provisions cannot be changed at all in individual contracts; dealing with these will require industrywide reforms of the kind advocated by the NWU.

---

[1] This chapter is adapted from the much more detailed *NWU Guide to Book Contracts* written by Philip Mattera and Maria Pallante. That document is available only to members of the NWU. Union members may also take advantage of the NWU's network of book contract advisors and book grievance officers.

# *Rights & Money*

### RIGHTS: **What rights are being granted to the publisher?**

There are three basic types of rights to consider:

- **Copyright** relates to the question of who is the author (and thus owner) of the work for legal purposes.
- **Publishing rights** are the terms under which the copyright holder authorizes the publisher to print and sell the work;
- **Subsidiary rights** are the terms under which the copyright holder authorizes the publisher or others to produce (or adapt) the work in forms other than the primary edition.

### COPYRIGHT

*Copyright is discussed at length in Part 1, page 7.*

Copyright consists of those rights and privileges guaranteed to the legal author of a work under federal law. These include, above all, the right to reproduce the work and the right to prepare derivative works. Under U.S. copyright law, the copyright in a literary work belongs to the person who writes the work from the moment the words are expressed in some fixed form. (The exceptions to this are situations in which the writer is creating the work as an employee or in which the writer agrees to sign over all rights to the work to the publisher.)

### PUBLISHING RIGHTS

Unless you are planning to self-publish, you as the copyright holder will need to find someone else to publish your book. In signing a book contract, what you are essentially doing is granting various rights to a publisher. These publishing rights (which derive from your copyright) are the terms under which that publisher can print and distribute your book.

There are three aspects of publishing rights to consider:

- **Format:** In most book contracts, the basic publishing right being granted by the author is the right to publish the work in an original hardcover edition. In some cases, the primary publisher will also want the right to issue the work in paperback and other formats.

When a publisher intends to publish both the hardcover and paperback versions of a work, it will propose what is known as a "hard-soft deal."

Agreeing to a hard-soft deal can be advantageous, as long as the size of the advance on royalties reflects the broader grant of rights, and the royalty rate for paperback copies is adequate.

- **Duration:** The customary practice in the United States is to allow the primary publisher to retain exclusive publishing rights for the duration of the work's copyright term (which is currently 50 years from the author's death), as long as the work is kept in print.

- **Geographical Scope:** The final issue for publishing rights is the extent of the geographical area in which the primary publisher is authorized to exercise those rights. Traditionally, the primary publisher would ask for the exclusive right to issue the work in the English language in the United States, its possessions, Canada, and the Philippines. Often the primary publisher would be granted the nonexclusive right to sell the English-language edition elsewhere in the world.

In recent years, publishers have sought to gain increasingly broader geographical rights, and in many cases they demand exclusive world rights in English—sometimes in all languages. As with the granting of hardcover and softcover rights, it may make sense for an author who is less experienced or working without an agent to give the publisher world rights, as long as the size of the advance and other money provisions reflect the greater profit potential the publisher thus achieves.

### Subsidiary Rights

For a discussion of subsidiary rights, see the section on royalties, below.

**PAYMENTS: How much money will you receive from the publisher, when will you receive it, and how will it be calculated?**

### ADVANCES

An advance is a series of payments that a publisher agrees to give to the author in exchange for the right to publish the book. The author is entitled to keep the advance even if the publisher does not sell a single copy of the work. Assuming copies are sold, the publisher credits the author's royalty account for so much per copy, according to the agreed-on royalty terms. Once the total reaches the amount of the advance—at which time the book is said to have "earned out" the advance—the publisher begins to make additional payments to the author.

When negotiating an advance, remember that for most authors, the advance is the only compensation they end up receiving for writing the book.

*Schedule of advance payments:* When you consider the minimum advance you can settle for, keep in mind that the amount is usually paid out in several installments. This is particularly relevant if you are negotiating a contract based on a proposal and sample chapters, and thus have not yet written the whole book. Unless you have other sources of income, the advance will have to take care of your living expenses (and research costs) for as long as it takes you to complete the manuscript.

The most common arrangement is for half of the total advance to be paid upon signing of the contract and the remainder to be paid upon acceptance of the completed manuscript.

**WARNING!**

**The advance is often the only money a writer makes on a book**

### ROYALTIES

These payments are calculated in two main ways. Either they are a percentage of the cover price of the book (the **"list"** or **"gross"** basis); or they are a percentage of the money received by the publisher after discounts are given to the bookselling retailer or wholesaler. The latter are known as royalties based on **net**, which may also be referred to as "the publisher's dollar receipts" or "net proceeds."

Royalties were traditionally paid on the cover price. Occasionally, a publisher would complain that this arrangement was too onerous for books whose production costs were high (e.g., heavily illustrated works or reference volumes) and insisted on paying net royalties. What started out as a rare situation has become common practice among smaller publishing houses, university presses, and even for some types of works put out by trade publishers. **When you accept net royalties, you are effectively cutting your income by at least 40 percent** (i.e., the amount of the discount given to booksellers) for copies sold through retail channels.

WARNING!

*Royalty rates:* The most common royalty schedules for hardcover trade books is as follows:

■ 10 percent of the list price on the first 5,000 copies sold;

■ 12$\frac{1}{2}$ percent on the next 5,000 copies;

■ 15 percent on all copies beyond that.

Paperback rights are of two types: "trade paperback" and "mass market." A **trade paperback** is the upscale softcover version, usually priced these days above $10 and sold primarily in bookstores. For some mysterious reason, trade paperback royalties are almost always lower than those for hardcover editions. Moreover, the breakpoints are steeper (i.e., you have to sell a lot more copies to get to a higher rate) and sometimes are not offered at all. The most common royalty rates for trade paperbacks are:

*For more precise data on royalties, see page 89.*

■ 7$\frac{1}{2}$ percent of the list price for the first 10,000–25,000 copies

■ 10 percent thereafter

Starting rates, however, will often be as low as 5 percent.

**Mass market editions** are the less expensive versions that usually have smaller page sizes and are sold in drugstores, newsstands, supermarkets, airports, and other outlets, as well as bookstores. There is much greater variation in royalty rates for mass-market paperbacks—they can start as low as 4 percent and go to 15 percent or more—and the breakpoints are usually much higher, with the first often set at 150,000 copies. (**Note:** Book contracts typically specify lower royalty rates for special categories of sales, including mail order, copies sold at a "deep discount," copies of the original edition sold abroad, and copies sold to book clubs.)

*Royalty statements:* These are the means by which the publisher reports to the author on the sales of the book and the receipt of subsidiary-rights income. They are supposed to be accompanied by a check for moneys due to the author. Trade book publishers usually issue statements semi-annually, while small houses and university presses usually do so annually. There is a lag of 60 to 120 days from the end of the royalty period to the date when the publisher is obliged to deliver the statement and make any payments.

Traditionally, royalty statements have done more to conceal than reveal. They are often cryptic documents that are not understood by most authors—or even by some agents.

In recent years, in part under pressure from writers' groups such as the NWU, some publishers have been revising their standard roy-

*Royalty statements often conceal more than they reveal*

alty forms and providing more of the relevant data. Some of these new forms are quite complicated, though they still usually leave out important information, including the size of the print run. In addition, publishers continue to insist on lag times of up to four months before royalty checks are sent out. Such delays are unjustified in an era of computerized accounting, but the industry has grown used to a practice that in effect gives publishers interest-free loans of authors' money.

It is usually not possible for an individual author to negotiate changes to a publisher's standard royalty form or the payment schedule; it will require industrywide reform.

**SUBSIDIARY RIGHTS: How will you and the publisher divide the money that comes from licenses granted to others to make use of the work in forms other than the original edition?**

The question relates to what are known as subsidiary rights. Since these uses of the work often account for the lion's share of the potential income, close attention should be paid to these provisions of your contract.

Deciding whether it is better to reserve—keep—various rights or grant them to the publisher is a complicated matter. Traditionally, it was standard practice to allow authors to reserve certain "secondary subsidiary rights" (British Commonwealth rights, foreign rights, movie/TV rights, and first serialization—i.e., the right to publish an excerpt from the work before the book comes out), but publishers increasingly want to have exclusive control over as many subsidiary rights as possible.

If you are an experienced author with a good agent, you should reserve as much as possible. On the other hand, if you are working without an agent, your chances of selling these rights independently are not good. Thus it would make sense for you to give control over their disposition to the publisher.

*Income splits:* If you have somehow managed to reserve all subsidiary rights, then there would be no need for a subsidiary rights clause in the contract. Otherwise, your contract will have a list of the various subsidiary rights that the primary publisher has the exclusive right to exploit. For each there will be an indication of how the proceeds from that right are going to be divided between you and the publisher. For most rights, publishers will ask that the income be split 50-50; when dealing with inexperienced authors, they often want this arrangement to apply to all rights.

Keep in mind that when the publisher sells subsidiary rights, it is essentially acting as your agent and ideally should only be entitled to a percentage similar to that taken by agents, namely 10 to 15 percent. This argument, unfortunately, is not taken seriously by publishers. However, for the secondary subsidiary rights listed above, it is not difficult for the average author to get a share above 50 percent and frequently one in the 85–90 percent range.

**Special attention should be paid to electronic rights,** which once were considered throwaways, lumped together with trivial items such as microfilming. But with the explosion of new electronic media—from CD-ROM to the Internet—these rights are now coveted by publishers seeking to find new ways to sell the same material.

The *NWU Guide to Book Contracts* has an extensive discussion of this subject. Basically the union argues that authors who have agents or personal contact with electronic publishers should try to

**WARNING!**

reserve electronic rights. If this is not possible, you should try to limit the electronic rights granted to the print publisher in terms of format and duration. You should also try to get a share of income from these rights that is well above 50 percent and try to get a right of approval over the granting of electronic licenses.

# The Manuscript

NATURE OF THE WORK: **What are the specifications of the manuscript you are promising to produce?**

The contract should give some indication of the nature of the work, or at least a tentative title. You may also wish to make your proposal a part of the contract.

While the agreement should always identify the estimated length of the manuscript to be delivered, as previously agreed on by the author and publisher, the word count should be specified as one that is approximate, to protect you if the manuscript turns out to be somewhat longer or shorter. Also, be sure the deadline you agree to is realistic.

SUPPLEMENTARY MATERIALS: **Who is responsible for obtaining and paying for illustrations and other supplementary material?**

Most contracts make it the responsibility of the author to supply supplementary materials such as photographs, artwork, charts, and graphs. If your book involves a substantial amount of such materials, try to get the publisher to share in the cost of their preparation.

*Permissions:* When you plan to make use in your book of material that is covered by someone else's copyright, you will usually need to get written permission to do so. Often the publisher of that material will charge you a fee.

Most publishers make it the responsibility of the author to secure permissions, and most also require the author to pay all related fees. If you expect to use little or no copyrighted material in your book, this is not an issue to be very concerned about. If, however, you are producing an anthology of numerous previously published pieces or a heavily illustrated work, the time and money involved in getting permissions can be quite substantial. In such cases **it is not reasonable for you to absorb all the permission costs, unless you are getting a large advance that was determined with permission costs in mind.**

**WARNING!**

## "UNACCEPTABLE MANUSCRIPT": What happens if the publisher does not like what you deliver?

Manuscript acceptance is one of the most contentious issues in book publishing. Numerous authors who sell books on the basis of a proposal find that when they later deliver the full manuscript, the publisher claims the work is unsatisfactory and demands repayment of the advance.

Although publishers sometimes take this position based on an honest opinion that the work is substandard, all too often rejections have nothing to do with the quality of the manuscript. Among the real reasons may be that the house has been acquired by another publisher and ordered to pare its list; that the acquiring editor has left the company and no one else is excited enough about the book to take primary responsibility for it; or that the subject of the work is not deemed as "hot" as it was when the contract was signed.

Ultimately, it is not possible to compel a publishing house to put out a work it does not wish to publish. The proper contract language can, however, make it more difficult for a house to reject a manuscript frivolously.

In addition, the right contract language can make it more difficult for a publishing house to demand repayment of the advance if it does end up rejecting the manuscript. **The NWU has long held that, if an author writes the book, the advance should be nonrefundable. To allow the house to recoup the advance is to take all risk out of the publishing contract for the publisher.** If the publisher genuinely does not like what the author has produced, then it should simply cancel the contract and write off the advance as a business loss. The industry, however, has strongly resisted this principle, so until industry-wide reforms can be enacted, authors will have to focus on the following contract fixes.

**NWU RECOMMENDS**

When a manuscript is deemed unsatisfactory, the contract should require the publisher to give a detailed statement in writing on exactly what is deemed deficient and to give the author an opportunity to revise the manuscript in a way that addresses the stated objections.

If the revised manuscript is also rejected, and the publisher insists on rejecting the work, then the author has to be concerned with getting back the publishing rights (reversion) and with the question of what happens to the advance.

*First-proceeds clauses:* These are a mechanism publishers have come up with to make repayment of advances less burdensome. They are not as desirable as language making advances nonrefundable, but they are often the best terms an author can get.

First-proceeds clauses allow authors to avoid having to refund the advance directly. Instead, the publisher frees the author to shop around the rejected manuscript to other houses. When the work is resold, then the first publisher is repaid out of the money received from the new publisher. A less desirable form of the first-proceeds clause states that if the work is not sold within a certain period (usually 12 months), then the author is obliged to repay the advance directly.

## EDITING AND PRODUCTION COSTS: What are your rights and responsibilities relating to the editing and production of the manuscript?

The contract should state clearly that the publisher is responsible for the costs of production. The publisher should arrange for the manuscript to be professionally copy edited, and the edited manuscript should be sent to you for review. Although the publisher will insist on language saying that the manuscript must conform to standards of spelling, grammar, etc., the contract should state that no substantial changes in the content of the work may be made without the consent of the author.

Once the work has been set in type, you will be sent proofs for review. Traditionally, the author would first receive galley sheets to review, and after those had been corrected, page proofs. Publisher contracts will typically require you to review proofs promptly. It is also common for contracts to state that the author is responsible for the cost of making author's alterations to the proofs, to the extent that such costs exceed 10 or 15 percent of the original cost of composition.

*Production decisions*: Publishers typically insist on controlling the details of production, distribution, pricing, and promotion. Over some of these issues—the cover price of the book, for example—it will be next to impossible for you to have any control. You should, however, try to negotiate at least a consultative role with respect to the creative decisions that will be made regarding the production of your book, especially the cover and dust jacket copy.

### FAILURE TO PUBLISH: What happens if the publisher does not publish the book?

Be sure that your contract includes a clause that requires the publisher to publish the book within a specified amount of time. A deadline of 12 months is best, though many publishers insist on 18 or 24 months. Should a publisher fail to publish by the end of that period, the author must have the right to terminate the contract unilaterally and recover all rights granted to the publisher. In such cases the author should retain any advances received.

### INDEMNIFICATION: What happens if someone sues you and the publisher?

It is not unreasonable for the publisher to ask that you promise that the work you are submitting is original, that it has not been previously published, that it does not infringe on someone else's copyright, and that you are free to grant the specified publishing rights. Most standard contracts will also ask the author to promise that the work is not obscene or libelous, and that it does not invade anyone's privacy.

All of this is known as the author's warranty, and it is usually presented together with what is known as an **indemnification clause**, which makes the author responsible for any legal expenses and damages resulting from lawsuits that involve violations of the above promises.

B
O
O
K
S

**WARNING!**

Standard contracts will typically require the author to cooperate with the publisher's lawyers in modifying passages that may be obscene, libelous, etc. That is reasonable, as is the provision that allows the publisher to cancel the contract if it turns out that the manuscript is not original or is otherwise unpublishable for legal reasons.

**What is not reasonable is sweeping language requiring you to pay the publisher's legal expenses in the event a lawsuit is brought.** Ideally, the contract will say that if you cooperate with the publisher's lawyers and modify the manuscript so that the lawyers think it will pass legal scrutiny, you should be free of all responsibility for legal expenses.

Publishers, supposedly concerned about those rare cases in which an author submits a completely plagiarized manuscript, usually insist on the inclusion of an indemnification clause. You might try to negotiate language that says you are responsible for legal expenses only when the plaintiff is successful, which means that you are not responsible for expenses relating to frivolous or unsuccessful claims.

*Libel insurance:* For any book that is investigative or controversial in nature, you should try to get coverage under the publisher's libel insurance policy. Beware of the deductibles contained in these policies, which may require an author to pay the first $50,000 or more in damages. Try to get the publisher to pay the deductible, or at least put a cap on your liability.

### ARBITRATION: What happens if you have a dispute with the publisher?

In most cases, authors who believe their contract has been violated by the publisher have only one legal option: to embark on costly and time-consuming court action. Since writers usually cannot afford to take this step, publishers will prevail by default. NWU members have recourse to the grievance committee, but even the union cannot always get publishers to do the right thing.

There is a more practical way for authors to seek justice, and that is through the system of arbitration. This is a process in which the parties to a contract agree to have any disputes heard by an impartial third party in a non-courtroom setting. The arbitrator then issues a ruling that is binding on the parties.

Some publishers agree to arbitration clauses in their author contracts as a matter of course, some will consent to the clause if the author requests it, and still others will never consent to it.

## The Future

**OPTION CLAUSES: Do you have to offer your next book to the same publisher?**

Option clauses (sometimes known as the right of first refusal) are provisions that give the publisher the right to consider your next book project before you show it to any other house. Ultimately, you cannot be compelled to sign a new contract with the same house, but the option provision can seriously encumber your ability to offer the new work to other publishers.

The most desirable alternative is to remove the option clause entirely—a step that many publishers will agree to without much resistance. Others will remain adamant about keeping the clause. In that case, you should try to modify the provision in various ways.

- Do not agree to an option clause that requires you to submit a complete manuscript to the publisher for consideration. Instead, agree only that you will submit a proposal for the new work.

- If you write in different genres, specify that the option clause will only apply to your next work in the same genre.

- Set a strict deadline (say, 30 days after submission) by which the publisher must make an offer on the new project.

- Do not agree to language that binds you to the same terms as the original contract, and do not consent to restrictions on your right to reject the publisher's offer in favor of another offer— even one that is less lucrative. There may be circumstances in which you decide it is best to go with a house that is offering less money but other terms that are more attractive.

NWU
RECOMMENDS

**Can the publisher bar you from publishing another book that might compete with the title it is issuing?**

Most book contracts have something called a competing works clause. This provision, which comes in various guises, is meant to prevent you from unfairly re-using the material from your book in a deal with another publisher.

The problem is that competing works clauses are often written in a way that can limit your career. The best alternative is to remove this clause entirely. If this is not possible, try to put a time limit on the restriction and limit the restriction to competing works on the same (not simply similar) subject.

**TERMINATION: What happens if your book is no longer available?**

The out-of-print (or termination) clause deals with the circumstances surrounding the decision of the publisher to take your book out of distribution.

If framed correctly, it can allow you to recapture rights from a publisher that may have failed to execute its responsibility of properly editing, packaging, and promoting a book. As it is often written, however, this clause can keep your book in limbo and make you wait years for a reversion of rights.

A proper termination clause will, first of all, clearly define **what it means for a work to be out of print**. Preferably, this should refer to availability of the book in its primary market. What this means is that the original publisher cannot claim the work is still in print if the only forms in which it is available are translations, audio cassette, etc.

Next, the clause should require the publisher to **notify you when it has decided to take the work out of print**. This commonsense requirement is, however, almost never found in publisher boilerplate. Instead, the typical language requires you to inquire about the status of the work. At that point, if the work is not available for sale, the publisher is usually given six months to decide whether to reprint it. It is only after that period of time that you are entitled to reclaim the rights, if the publisher has not taken steps to reprint the work.

**WARNING!**

**REVISED EDITIONS:** What happens if your publisher wants you to do a revised edition of the book?

Ideally, the contract you sign for a book will apply only to the original edition of the work; a revised edition would require a new agreement. This would give you an opportunity to negotiate better royalty rates if the book is doing well. It could also allow you to get a new advance, which would be quite important if the revision is going to be time-consuming.

If this is not possible, try to get a clause that requires a new contract if the amount of revision exceeds a certain portion (say, 25 percent) of the original text. Also, for works that could be revised regularly, try to prevent the publisher from having complete control over the frequency of the new editions. If the revisions are expected to be less extensive and less frequent, then it may be difficult to avoid language that states that revised editions will be subject to the same contract terms as the original edition.

**If so, be sure that the contract states that the deadline for the submission of the revisions is to be determined by the mutual consent of you and the publisher, to avoid the imposition of unreasonable timetables.**

NWU
RECOMMENDS

# Book Rates & Practices

In the unregulated, irregular world of freelance writing, no market is as capricious as that for book writing. Book publishing is largely a subjective industry. The decision to publish a book is based on the editor's taste and the publisher's guess of the book's market potential. That same guess, along with the publisher's drive to make a profit, dictates the terms of the publishing contract. A book considered a potential hot seller will command a six- or even seven-figure advance, a large print run, and a serious promotional budget, while a book deemed of limited interest is likely to bring its author an advance of a few thousand dollars, a small print run, and no money for promotion.

In such an environment, it is difficult to generalize about what is a good publishing deal. Is a $20,000 advance reasonable? It may be for a mass-market paperback[1] with a print run of 50,000; it is not for a hardcover with a run of 20,000. You have to try to get the best possible terms for your contract.

In thinking about book publishing deals, it is important to keep in mind that there are a great many differences among publishers. What might be a good offer from a small press, for instance, is generally grossly inadequate if offered by a large trade house. And since there are so many intangibles that go into a publishing contract and the experience itself, you have to be clear about your primary concerns and the trade offs you are willing to make to satisfy these. A large publisher, for example, may offer a bigger advance but would not give you the kind of editorial attention you want. A smaller press, on the other hand, might not have the resources to promote your book aggressively.

*Details on contracts: page 67.*

---

[1]It is important to differentiate between *trade* paperbacks and *mass market* paperbacks. Trade paperbacks are the upscale softcover editions that sell for $10 to $15. Mass market paperbacks are the less expensive books often sold for $4 to $7 in drugstores, supermarkets, newsstands, etc.

**B**
**O**
**O**
**K**
**S**

This chapter presents information that will give you a general idea of the conditions common in the book marketplace. The recommendations made by the NWU here are meant to serve as guides in dealing with some of the tangible and intangible issues that come up in considering a contract.

The information is divided by type of book—trade fiction and nonfiction[2], mass-market paperbacks, children's books, textbooks, and professional books.

## *Advances*[3]

### AMOUNTS

Three pieces of information about advance amounts are provided: (1) minimum and maximum reported advances; (2) the average advance; and (3) the prevalent range of advances in the marketplace (the range where most mid-list advances fall).

| ADVANCES: TRADE BOOKS | Min/max | Average | Prevalent range |
|---|---|---|---|
| **Fiction Hardcover** | $5,000/100,000 | $19,745 | $5,000—20,000 |
| **Fiction Paperback** | $1,500/56,000 | $14,135 | $1,500—5,000 |
| **Nonfiction Hardcover** | $5,000/150,000 | $20,560 | $10,000—50,000 |
| **Nonfiction Paperback** | $1,000/100,000 | $11,730 | $1,000—10,000 |

To put these numbers in perspective, we can look at the findings of The Authors Guild's 1988–1989 survey of trade-book authors. That survey showed that 47.4 percent of authors received advances of less than $20,000, 19.6 percent received between $20,000 and $40,000, and 32.8 percent received more than $40,000.

---

[2]We consider all books intended for a *general* adult audience trade books.
[3]All discussion of advances is based on data for mid-list authors

Although it is not unusual for small presses and university presses to offer no advances to authors, larger trade houses always pay advances, and certainly should be expected to do so.

**ADVANCES**

| | Min/max | Average | Prevalent range |
|---|---|---|---|
| **MASS MARKET PAPERBACKS** | | | |
| **Mystery** | $5,000/50,000 | $13,900 | $5,000—35,000 |
| **Romance** | $1,000/40,000 | $6,400 | $1,000—10,000 |
| **Science Fiction** | $3,500/40,000 | $19,900 | $7,500—40,000 |
| **Western** | $1,500/35,000 | $5,700 | $1,500—10,000 |
| **Young Adult** | $1,000/14,000 | $6,100 | $2,000—7,500 |
| **Other Original Paperback** | $1,500/35,000 | $10,500 | $1,500—10,000 |
| **CHILDREN'S BOOKS** | $0/53,000 | $5,061 | $0—7,000 |
| **TEXTBOOKS** | | | |
| **Elementary, Junior High & High School** | $0/5,000 | $1,500 | $0—1,500 |
| **College** | $0/50,000 | $5,350 | $0—10,000 |
| **Graduate** | $0/10,000 | $2,650 | $0—10,000 |
| **PROFESSIONAL BOOKS** | $0/20,000 | $4,200 | $0—10,000 |

B
O
O
K
S

## SCHEDULE OF ADVANCE PAYMENTS

The schedule of advance payments is a serious consideration in contract negotiations. Advances are paid out in installments, and it is important to make sure that you get as much of the money up front as possible.

The most common payment schedule for writers is half on signing and half on acceptance of the manuscript. NWU writers' survey respondents indicated that this is the prevalent payment schedule in the marketplace.

|  | ½ on signing,<br>½ on acceptance |
|---|---|
| **TRADE BOOKS** | |
| **Fiction Hardcover** | 87% |
| **Fiction Paperback** | 82% |
| **Nonfiction Hardcover** | 92.5% |
| **Nonfiction Paperback** | 91% |
| **MASS MARKET BOOKS** | |
| **Mystery** | 90% |
| **Romance** | 92% |
| **Science Fiction** | 81% |
| **Western** | 89% |
| **Young Adult** | 94% |
| **Other Original Paperback** | 86% |
| **CHILDREN'S BOOKS** | 97% |

SCHEDULE OF ADVANCE PAYMENTS

|  | ½ on signing, ½ on acceptance |
|---|---|
| **TEXTBOOKS** | |
| **Elementary, Junior High & High School** | 86% |
| **College** | 63% |
| **Graduate** | 75% |
| **PROFESSIONAL BOOKS** | 94% |

**NWU Recommends** ★ — Try not to accept less than 50% of the advance on signing, and no part on publication (unless you got a huge advance). If your contract stipulates a three-part payout, the second should be for "substantial progress," the third on completion.

EARNING OUT THE ADVANCE

The advance you get for your book is just that: an advance against the royalties you are expected to make on sales of the book. As copies of your book are sold, royalties are credited toward the advance you received. You get no royalties until the advance is "earned out."

| TRADE BOOKS | Earned out | Did not earn out | Unknown |
|---|---|---|---|
| **Fiction Hardcover** | 39% | 52% | 9% |
| **Fiction Paperback** | 36% | 57% | 7% |
| **Nonfiction Hardcover** | 46% | 43% | 11% |
| **Nonfiction Paperback** | 50% | 40% | 10% |

| EARNING OUT THE ADVANCE | Earned out | Did not earn out | Unknown |
|---|---|---|---|
| **MASS MARKET BOOKS** | | | |
| **Mystery** | 60% | 40% | 0% |
| **Romance** | 50% | 50% | 0% |
| **Science Fiction** | 60% | 35% | 5% |
| **Western** | 58% | 42% | 0% |
| **Young Adult** | 50% | 25% | 25% |
| **Other Original Paperback** | 41% | 55% | 4% |
| **CHILDREN'S BOOKS** | 43% | 41% | 16% |
| **TEXTBOOKS** | | | |
| **Elementary, Junior High & High School** | 80% | 20% | 0% |
| **College** | 61% | 22% | 17% |
| **Graduate** | 40% | 20% | 40% |
| **PROFESSIONAL BOOKS** | 64% | 23% | 13% |

As you can see, many books' chances of earning out their advances are fairly low. The reasons for not earning out are complex and numerous, from intense competition for shelf space to inadequate promotion to premature remaindering. What is important to understand is that most of these reasons are outside of your control and that a book's sales performance is generally not a very realistic gauge of its quality.

Whatever these reasons, however, it seems clear that **it is in most writers' best interests to negotiate for as much of an advance as possible.** (This is especially true if you are selling a proposal and will need the advance money to support yourself while you are writing the book.)

# Royalties

### RATES

Royalties are calculated as a percentage of sales, usually with the rate going up as more copies are sold. In negotiating contracts, it is important to **consider** both the **royalty rate** and the **escalations**—the points at which rates go up—as well as the **method used to calculate royalties**—list price or publisher's net. The rate and the method of calculation can be used as counterbalancing negotiation points—e.g., if you are getting royalties based on publishers' net, hold out for higher rates.

It is essential that you are clear about the NWU recommendations for minimum royalty rates. **The ranges given on the following pages are suggestions for the lowest rates you should consider; if you can get more,** *do it.*

## ROYALTY RATES: TRADE BOOKS

For trade books, standard escalations are: (1) for hardcovers: first 5,000 copies, next 5,000 copies, and all copies thereafter; (2) for paperbacks: first 10,000 copies and all copies thereafter.

| | Prevalent Range | NWU Recommends (at least) |
|---|---|---|
| **FICTION** | | |
| **Hardcover** | | |
| First 5,000 books | 5—10% | 10—15% |
| Next 5,000 books | 10—12% | 12.5—15% |
| Thereafter | 12—15% | 15—20% |
| **Paperback** | | |
| First 10,000 books | 5—10% | 7—10% |
| Thereafter | 8—15% | 10—15% |
| **NONFICTION** | | |
| **Hardcover** | | |
| First 5,000 books | 5—10% | 10—15% |
| Next 5,000 books | 10—15% | 12.5—15% |
| Thereafter | 10—15% | 15—20% |
| **Paperback** | | |
| First 10,000 | 5—10% | 7—10% |
| Thereafter | 8—15% | 10—15% |

The Authors Guild reports that their 1988–1989 survey showed that 58.1 percent of authors received the most common royalty, while 14.8 percent received more favorable terms, and 17.4 percent less favorable ones.

## ROYALTY RATES:
## MASS MARKET BOOKS

For mass market books, escalations tend to be at very high points, with the first often set at 150,000 copies. No matter how astronomical the numbers may be, however, it is essential to make sure that your contract specifies some escalations.

|  | Prevalent Range | NWU Recommends (at least) |
|---|---|---|
| **MYSTERY** | | |
| **First 150,000 books** | 6—15% | 7—15% |
| **Thereafter** | 8—15% | 10—15% |
| **ROMANCE** | | |
| **First 150,000 books** | 4—10% | 7—15% |
| **Thereafter** | 7—15% | 10—15% |
| **SCIENCE FICTION** | | |
| **First 150,000 books** | 7—10% | 7—15% |
| **Thereafter** | 8—15% | 10—15% |
| **WESTERN** | | |
| **First 150,000 books** | 2—10% | 7—15% |
| **Thereafter** | 4—15% | 10—15% |
| **YOUNG ADULT** | | |
| **First 150,000 books** | 1—10% | 7—15% |
| **Thereafter** | 1—12% | 10—15% |
| **OTHER ORIGINAL PAPERBACK** | | |
| **First 150,000 books** | 5—15% | 7—15% |
| **Thereafter** | 7—15% | 10—15% |

## ROYALTY RATES:
## CHILDREN'S BOOKS

For children's books, common escalations are: first 5,000 copies, next 5,000 copies, and all copies thereafter.

|  | Prevalent Range | NWU Recommends (at least) |
|---|---|---|
| **First 5,000 books** | 2—8% | 7—10% |
| **Next 5,000 books** | 5—10% | 8—12.5% |
| **Thereafter** | 8—15% | 12.5—15% |

## PROFESSIONAL BOOKS

For professional books, escalations tend to be: first 5,000 copies, next 5,000 copies, and all copies thereafter.

Because it is common that royalty rates for professional books are based on publisher's net, we have set recommended royalty rates higher.

|  | Prevalent Range | NWU Recommends (at least) |
|---|---|---|
| **First 5,000** | 4—7% | 10—12.5% |
| **Next 5,000** | 8—10% | 12.5—15% |
| **Thereafter** | 10—15% | 15—20% |

**ROYALTY RATES:**
**TEXTBOOKS**

Common escalations for textbooks are: first 5,000 copies, next 5,000 copies, and all copies thereafter.

| | Prevalent Range | NWU Recommends (at least) |
|---|---|---|
| **ELEMENTARY, JUNIOR HIGH & HIGH SCHOOL** | | |
| **First 5,000 books** | 5—8% | 7—10% |
| **Next 5,000 books** | 7—10% | 10—15% |
| **Thereafter** | 10—15% | 12—20% |
| **COLLEGE** | | |
| **First 5,000 books** | 7—10% | 7—10% |
| **Next 5,000 books** | 8—12% | 10—15% |
| **Thereafter** | 10—19% | 12—20% |
| **GRADUATE** | | |
| **First 5,000 books** | 5—10% | 7—10% |
| **Next 5,000 books** | 7—11% | 10—15% |
| **Thereafter** | 10-15% | 12—20% |

## ROYALTY CALCULATIONS

As we have noted, royalties can be calculated as a percentage of the book's list price or of the amount received by the publisher after discounts—publisher's net. Clearly, royalties based on list price are more advantageous for authors.

|  | List Price | Publisher's Net |
|---|---|---|
| **TRADE BOOKS** | | |
| **Fiction Hardcover** | 95% | 5% |
| **Fiction Paperback** | 89% | 11% |
| **Nonfiction Hardcover** | 77% | 23% |
| **Nonfiction Paperback** | 74% | 26% |
| **MASS MARKET BOOKS** | | |
| **Mystery** | 96% | 4% |
| **Romance** | 82% | 18% |
| **Science Fiction** | 91% | 9% |
| **Western** | 89% | 11% |
| **Young Adult** | 80% | 20% |
| **Other Original Paperback** | 84% | 16% |
| **CHILDREN'S BOOKS** | 85% | 15% |
| **TEXTBOOKS** | | |
| **Elementary, Junior High & High School** | 29% | 71% |
| **College** | 57% | 43% |
| **Graduate** | 45% | 56% |
| **PROFESSIONAL BOOKS** | 47% | 53% |

## TIMELY PAYMENTS

Provided that your book earns out its advance, you are entitled to receive your royalty payments from the publisher on a timely, regular basis. Publishers generally send out royalty payments together with royalty statements at the end of each accounting cycle—every six months for trade publishers and every 12 months for academic and small-press publishers. Royalty statements and payments are supposed to be issued 60 to 120 days after the end of the accounting period.

The NWU believes that, in this day of computerized accounting, **writers should not have to wait more than 30 to 60 days after an accounting period—which could be as much as 14 months after sale—to receive their royalty payments.** The union's book campaign, as well as agents' groups, are working to improve this situation.

NWU
RECOMMENDS

## RESERVES AGAINST RETURNS

The book publishing and selling industry's system of returns, whereby book stores return unsold copies of books to the publisher for a full refund, creates a great deal of financial uncertainty. Publishers pass on a portion of that uncertainty to authors by holding a percentage of royalties in one royalty accounting period as reserves against possible returns in the next period.

The main problem with this system is that it is based on the premise that a set of unlikely circumstances—a large volume of orders for a book with a relatively small advance and heavy returns many months after the original orders—is actually common. Publishers routinely keep reserves for just about all of their books, essentially getting enormous interest-free loans from the authors.

**The NWU holds that the practice of holding returns against reserved for all titles should be abolished.**

This will not happen overnight. In the meantime, make sure that your contract does not just give the publisher the right to withhold a "reasonable" reserve for returns. The contract should spell out the limit of the reserve and the number of accounting periods that reserves can be withheld. The NWU recommends limiting reserves to no more than 15 percent for hardcovers and trade paperbacks and 30 percent for mass market paperbacks; reserves should be held for no more than two accounting periods.

NWU
RECOMMENDS

### ACCURACY OF ROYALTIES

Royalty statements are notoriously obscure. They generally omit such pertinent information as the number of copies printed and tend to give only murky details about how the book is selling.

Moreover, many authors and authors' organizations have long had reason to suspect that the information in the royalty statements is inaccurate—and that authors are not receiving payments for books sold. The recent well-publicized dispute between Judith Applebaum, the author of *How to Get Happily Published*, and HarperCollins is a case in point. HarperCollins, claiming to be unable to provide the information requested by the auditors, agreed to pay Applebaum $7,176.81 in back royalties, as well as her legal and audit expenses.

**We recommend, therefore, that your contract include a clause allowing you to audit the publisher's records on your book.**

NWU
RECOMMENDS

## *Rights*

---

**COPYRIGHT HOLDER**

We asked writers who holds the copyright to their published books. The results are presented as percentages of respondents.

| TRADE BOOKS | Author | Publisher |
|---|---|---|
| **Fiction Hardcover** | 89.6% | 10.4% |
| **Fiction Paperback** | 86% | 14% |
| **Nonfiction Hardcover** | 85% | 15% |
| **Nonfiction Paperback** | 80% | 20% |

---

B
O
O
K
S

| COPYRIGHT HOLDER | Author | Publisher |
|---|---|---|
| **MASS MARKET BOOKS** | | |
| **Mystery** | 91% | 9% |
| **Romance** | 82% | 18% |
| **Science Fiction** | 80% | 20% |
| **Western** | 84% | 16% |
| **Young Adult** | 74% | 26% |
| **Other Original Paperback** | 81% | 19% |
| **CHILDREN'S BOOKS** | 84.7% | 15.3% |
| **TEXTBOOKS** | | |
| **Elementary, Junior High & High School** | 57% | 43% |
| **College** | 68% | 32% |
| **Graduate** | 80% | 20% |
| **PROFESSIONAL BOOKS** | 56% | 44% |

These statistics are really unsettling. Copyright is your assurance of being able to reproduce the work and to derive income from it. By signing over the copyright, you give up your rights as the owner of the work.

Copyright ownership is usually not an issue with trade publishers. Academic presses and small-press publishers, however, often pressure authors to sign over the copyright. This is exploitative, and you should never agree to such terms. Writers get paid little enough, at the very least you should make sure that you can resell your work if the opportunity presents itself.

**Authors should always retain copyright.**

NWU
RECOMMENDS

*More on subsidiary rights: page 72.*

**B
O
O
K
S**

## SUBSIDIARY RIGHTS

Subsidiary rights are those that govern the production of the work in forms other than the primary edition, such as paperback editions, electronic editions, dramatization (movie/TV), translation, merchandising, etc. Subsidiary rights often account for most of the income derived from a book. Therefore, it is essential to pay careful attention to the grant of subsidiary rights in your contract.

---

**SUBSIDIARY RIGHTS HANDLED BY PUBLISHER**

**TRADE BOOKS**

| | First Serialization | Dramatization | British Commonwealth | Foreign Translation | Merchandising/ Commercial |
|---|---|---|---|---|---|
| **Fiction Hardcover** | 64% | 26% | 32% | 31% | 29% |
| **Fiction Paperback** | 50% | 24% | 37% | 52% | 35% |
| **Nonfiction Hardcover** | 63% | 34% | 56% | 57% | 39% |
| **Nonfiction Paperback** | 67% | 39% | 51% | 57% | 48% |

**MASS MARKET BOOKS**

| | First Serialization | Dramatization | British Commonwealth | Foreign Translation | Merchandising/ Commercial |
|---|---|---|---|---|---|
| **Mystery** | 67% | 50% | 67% | 75% | 50% |
| **Romance** | 70% | 65% | 62% | 69% | 62% |
| **Science Fiction** | 67% | 58% | 33% | 33% | 33% |
| **Western** | 65% | 52% | 37% | 56% | 30% |
| **Young Adult** | 42% | 25% | 42% | 46% | 27% |
| **Other Original Paperback** | 86% | 42% | 67% | 79% | 43% |

---

## SUBSIDIARY RIGHTS HANDLED BY PUBLISHER

| | First Serialization | Dramatization | British Commonwealth | Foreign Translation | Merchandising/ Commercial |
|---|---|---|---|---|---|
| **CHILDREN'S BOOKS** | 65% | 53% | 57% | 56% | 46% |
| **TEXTBOOKS** | | | | | |
| **Elementary, Junior High & High School** | 50% | 50% | 67% | 67% | 50% |
| **College** | 27% | 20% | 73% | 92% | 20% |
| **Graduate** | 50% | 50% | 75% | 75% | 50% |
| **PROFESSIONAL BOOKS** | 31% | 18% | 31% | 53% | 31% |

B
O
O
K
S

## SUBSIDIARY RIGHTS SALES: DID PUBLISHERS DO AN ADEQUATE JOB?

We also asked authors how adept their publishers are at selling those subsidiary rights which they handle.

| | Yes | No |
|---|---|---|
| **TRADE BOOKS** | | |
| **Fiction Hardcover** | 41% | 59% |
| **Fiction Paperback** | 58% | 42% |
| **Nonfiction Hardcover** | 34% | 66% |
| **Nonfiction Paperback** | 41% | 59% |

## SUBSIDIARY RIGHTS SALES: DID PUBLISHERS DO AN ADEQUATE JOB?

|  | Yes | No |
|---|---|---|
| **MASS MARKET BOOKS** | | |
| **Mystery** | 25% | 75% |
| **Romance** | 34% | 66% |
| **Science Fiction** | 50% | 50% |
| **Western** | 46% | 54% |
| **Young Adult** | 29% | 71% |
| **Other Original Paperback** | 23% | 77% |
| **CHILDREN'S BOOKS** | 37% | 63% |
| **TEXTBOOKS** | | |
| **Elementary, Junior High & High School** | 75% | 25% |
| **College** | 36% | 64% |
| **Graduate** | 80% | 20% |
| **PROFESSIONAL BOOKS** | 20% | 80% |

# Print Runs

The number of copies printed—the print run—is a function of that same guess as to the book's market potential that we talked about in the beginning of this chapter. If the print run is large, the publisher expects the book to do well and is more likely to support it with aggressive promotions and sales efforts. In general, publishers tend to reserve large print runs for blockbusters, preferring to reprint if a book proves to be a hot seller.

The information below will give you a good idea of the print run you can expect for your book.

| PRINT RUN | Min/max | Average | Prevalent range |
|---|---|---|---|
| **TRADE BOOKS** | | | |
| **Fiction Hardcover** | 500/72,000 | 15,600 | 5,000—30,000 |
| **Fiction Paperback** | 750/500,000 | 40,600 | 5,000—30,000 |
| **Nonfiction Hardcover** | 800/100,000 | 15,000 | 5,000—30,000 |
| **Nonfiction Paperback** | 500/300,000 | 18,000 | 5,000—30,000 |
| **MASS MARKET BOOKS** | | | |
| **Mystery** | 5,000/150,000 | 56,500 | 25,000—80,000 |
| **Romance** | 10,000/500,000 | 65,000 | 25,000—100,000 |
| **Science Fiction** | 5,000/150,000 | 55,000 | 25,000—75,000 |
| **Western** | 5,000/100,000 | 25,000 | 10,000—50,000 |
| **Young Adult** | 10,000/150,000 | 47,500 | 25,000—70,000 |
| **Other Original Paperback** | 3,000/250,000 | 54,300 | 25,000—75,000 |

| PRINT RUN | | | |
|---|---|---|---|
| | Min/max | Average | Prevalent range |
| **CHILDREN'S BOOKS** | 500/70,000 | 11,500 | 5,000—10,000 |
| **TEXTBOOKS** | | | |
| **Elementary, Junior High & High School** | 5,000/100,000 | 20,000 | 5,000—50,000 |
| **College** | 850/50,000 | 15,000 | 3,000—20,000 |
| **Graduate** | 3,000/60,000 | 16,200 | 3,000—10,000 |
| **PROFESSIONAL BOOKS** | 400/60,000 | 12,000 | 3,000—10,000 |

A caveat must be added here. **Often authors do not know the actual print run of their books, since publishers are reluctant to provide that information.**

## Editing

We were pleased to find out that most authors seem satisfied with the editorial attention their books receive (from 64 to 92 percent of authors in all categories in the NWU survey said editing was adequate). However, we increasingly hear complaints that editors are overworked and books do not receive adequate attention from them.

# *Promotion*

Among the most common complaints authors have is that their books are not sufficiently promoted to help sales. The blockbuster mentality dominant in the publishing industry encourages a highly uneven distribution of marketing and promotion budgets, with most of the money going to pitch the few books that publishers pay huge advances for, produce in large quantities, and fulfill their expectations of bestsellerdom.

| ADEQUATE PROMOTION AND MARKETING? | | |
|---|---|---|
| | Yes | No |
| **TRADE BOOKS** | | |
| **Fiction Hardcover** | 47% | 53% |
| **Fiction Paperback** | 72% | 28% |
| **Nonfiction Hardcover** | 44% | 56% |
| **Nonfiction Paperback** | 46% | 54% |
| **MASS MARKET BOOKS** | | |
| **Mystery** | 33% | 68% |
| **Romance** | 28% | 72% |
| **Science Fiction** | 55% | 45% |
| **Western** | 47% | 53% |
| **Young Adult** | 60% | 40% |
| **Other Original Paperback** | 23% | 77% |

| ADEQUATE PROMOTION AND MARKETING? | | |
|---|---|---|
| | Yes | No |
| **CHILDREN'S BOOKS** | 67% | 33% |
| **TEXTBOOKS** | | |
| **Elementary, Junior High & High School** | 89% | 11% |
| **College** | 52% | 48% |
| **Graduate** | 22% | 78% |
| **PROFESSIONAL BOOKS** | 46% | 54% |

# Remaindering

There comes a point in the life of most books when the publisher decides that it is no longer worth its while to carry the book. At that point, the publisher stops publication and sells the remaining copies—the book is *remaindered*. Sometimes, the publisher will remainder part of the inventory of a slow-selling title, while simultaneously selling it at full price. A book can be remaindered before it goes out of print.

The timing of remaindering varies, depending on how a book is selling and each publisher's predilection. The author has little leverage in affecting this decision. In general, contracts specify that—at least theoretically—books cannot go out of print (and therefore be remaindered) in less than one or two years after publication.

# Agents

The word on the street is that it has become close to impossible to get a trade book published without an agent. We wanted to find out how true this is, and also asked about the need for agents in other genres.

*More on agents: page 115.*

**B
O
O
K
S**

| AGENTS | Represented | Not represented |
|---|---|---|
| **TRADE BOOKS** | | |
| **Fiction Hardcover** | 79% | 21% |
| **Fiction Paperback** | 60% | 40% |
| **Nonfiction Hardcover** | 63% | 37% |
| **Nonfiction Paperback** | 49% | 51% |
| **MASS MARKET BOOKS** | | |
| **Mystery** | 69% | 31% |
| **Romance** | 62% | 38% |
| **Science Fiction** | 88% | 12% |
| **Western** | 59% | 41% |
| **Young Adult** | 47% | 53% |
| **Other Original Paperback** | 60% | 40% |
| **CHILDREN'S BOOKS** | 68% | 32% |

B
O
O
K
S

| AGENTS | | |
|---|---|---|
| | Represented | Not represented |
| **TEXTBOOKS** | | |
| **Elementary, Junior High & High School** | 8% | 92% |
| **College** | 24% | 76% |
| **Graduate** | 15% | 85% |
| **PROFESSIONAL BOOKS** | 12.5% | 87.5% |

# Writing With and For Others:
# *Ghostwriting & Collaborating*

BY CATHERINE REVLAND

For the past 15 years, I have made my living ghostwriting trade books, primarily for celebrities, and nearly always without credit on the cover. "And these people take full credit?" other writers say, their voices rising in indignation. "That's dishonest!" More sympathetic types wonder about my psychological state, suggesting that perhaps I should go into therapy to explore why I would choose such a self-effacing way to make a living.

Success has changed all that. A book I ghostwrote sold over 200,000 copies in paperback and has been issued in hardcover. The "author" is busy promoting the hardcover and the second book "we" are now writing.

Of course, it would be nice to get my name on the cover. But 50 percent of handsome royalties in the bank can go a long way to assuage the disappointment.

The business of selling books has become one of mass-marketable names—recognizable names, with no unfamiliar ones trailing behind attached by prepositions. What's in a celebrity name? Lots of advertising and promotion money. Quite frankly, as far as the publisher is concerned, your name does not add anything to the sales potential of the book. In fact, the promotion people do not want to know about the celebrity's need for a ghostwriter. It's like hearing of a star athlete's reliance on steroids: they hope it isn't so.

But do not get depressed. Although the phenomenon of the celebrity book elevates the status of writers no more than it does the status of literature, it means a lot of work for professional book writers and a good opportunity to make some real money.

The following will help you strike better collaboration and ghostwriting deals.

# Contract Points

## THE LETTER OF AGREEMENT

Negotiations are best begun at the initial meeting, when author and writer are usually brought together by an agent, editor, or referral. This is the time, especially for people who have not published, to get clear about what it means to hire a book writer and what it means to get published. If at the end of the meeting a collaboration seems possible, a letter of agreement can be drawn up. It should cover the following points:

### CREDIT

Insist on credit on the cover and spine of the book. Clearly specify what anonymity will cost you in terms of lost name recognition, professional status, and referrals.

- If you fail to get credit, insist on 50 percent of the royalties as a tradeoff for giving 100 percent of the credit to your co-author (see "Royalties," page 110). However, the publishing contract should identify the writer as "the writer" and the client as "the author." **The contract must be signed by both parties. Without this stipulation, your relationship can easily slip into work for hire.** For instance, if you are not party to the publishing contract, you will not receive your own royalty statements.

  It is also a good idea to have the contract stipulate that you will be referred to as "the writer" on the title page or, at the very least, in the Acknowledgments. Without the protection of such a clause, I have been credited in ways that made my contribution sound more like moral support, or as that of a humble drone who corrected the punctuation. The Acknowledgments are your best referral for future ghostwriting jobs—outside of cover credit, of course.

- If you do receive credit, everything that applies to negotiating a ghostwriting contract still applies, except it is now a **collaboration**. Still, your contract should designate you "the writer" and the person with whom you are collaborating, "the author," since each of your obligations will be different.

### DIVISION OF RESPONSIBILITIES

The letter of agreement should make it clear how the responsibilities are to be divided between you and the "author." Although you are probably going to do most of the writing, the agreement should specify what the "author" is required to provide you in terms of documents, access to human sources (letters of introduction, etc.), and, perhaps most important, adequate time for you to interview the "author." You should not be expected to gather the facts, ideas, anecdotes, etc., that the "author" wants in the book by means of telepathy.

It should also be made clear who is responsible for your various expenses while writing the book.

### RESOLUTION OF DISPUTES

When you first make the deal with the "author," relations between the two of you are bound to be quite amicable. While you hope it will remain that way, all too many collaborations end in ugly disputes. Unless you have carefully worded language in your letter of agreement, you could end up out of the picture, with little to show for your work. The letter of agreement should anticipate the following possibilities:

- If the relationship ends while you are writing the proposal, or after the proposal is completed but before the book is being written, you should get paid the full amount agreed on for the proposal, plus, if possible, additional money to compensate you for your removal from the project.

- If a publishing contract has been signed, and you are a party to it, you cannot be unilaterally removed from the project. The contract would have to be canceled and a settlement negotiated. Even if you are not a party to the publishing contract, you should insist on a substantial settlement, the size of which should reflect the amount of the book you have written by the time of the "divorce."

Probably the best all-purpose provision in the letter of agreement would be one that says, first, that you cannot be removed from the project without just cause. This would most likely not allow you to remain on the project with an "author" who has turned against you, but it will strengthen your hand with regard to the second provision, which should say that you cannot under any circumstances be removed from the project until you and the "author" have reached agreement on compensating you.

### THE ADVANCE

Experience has taught me to tell prospective clients that I cannot write a publishable, salable collaboration in less than a year, from proposal writing to final copyedit, and that it normally takes six months to produce a first draft. During this time, I must work full time to meet the deadline and must be fully compensated. I make it clear that the deadline is my deadline—the project ends when the money runs out and I have to take on another full time project. Save yourself months of anguish, frustration, and financial struggle as you underwrite the book with your own money by specifying a time frame in the initial letter of agreement. I have Carpel Tunnel Syndrome today because of all the extra writing I took on to support myself while I finished ghosting a book after the advance ran out.

Advise the author as to what a reasonable advance might be. These days, unless you are dealing with a big celebrity, six-figure advances are rare indeed. Explain to your prospective collaborator how much money you will require for a year's work—say a modest $30,000—and make it clear that if your share of the first half of the advance is not sufficient to cover that amount, he or she must make up the difference. In addition, "the author" must pay for your travel and transcribing expenses, which can be considerable. Using our very modest figure of $30,000 for the year, it becomes obvious that unless the advance is larger than $60,000, you will need the entire first installment of the advance in order to write the book.

Your collaborator can then receive the second half of the advance.

## ROYALTIES

If your author is a celebrity, or has the potential of becoming one, you may be in the blessed position of having an annuity in years to come if the book is a success. In general, a book has to sell in five figures before you begin receiving royalties.

At the initial meeting, negotiate with the knowledge that you quite likely will never see a penny in royalties. Do not, however, agree to accept less than 50% of the royalties. If your client insists on a bigger share, point out how much work you will be putting into the book for modest compensation and suggest that the prospect of half the royalties is a great incentive to produce the best book possible.

## THE PROPOSAL

I usually negotiate proposals as two-month projects for which I must be paid. The author may balk, but it is absurd to work on spec. If necessary, the client can be reimbursed for the fee you receive for the proposal out of the first royalties—not the advance, since you might need all of that to write the book.

## AGENTS: ONE OR TWO?

I have had the best luck getting a fair deal when the collaboration came through my own agent, or a referral I brought to my agent. In such cases, one agent works well for both author and writer, plus you split the agent's commission. Publishers and editors also prefer one agent, as two can be cumbersome to deal with. However, if the client already has an agent, I strongly suggest that you bring your own agent in on the deal, to have someone to look out for your interests and negotiate the agreement.

## RELATIONSHIP WITH EDITORS

Be sure to develop a direct working relationship with the editor assigned to the project. The senior editor may meet with the "author" alone at a swank French restaurant, but the hands-on editor needs to know who is cranking out the drafts. It also works to the editors' advantage.

There is this bittersweet aspect to the "as-told-to" craft: the more the book sounds like the author wrote it, the better you are as a ghostwriter. "Does not bear the mark of a ghostwriter," read *The New York Times* review of my greatest celebrity triumph. But the editors knew, and that is how a ghosting reputation is built.

# In Case of Success

It is every writer's dream to hit it big. Images of fat royalty checks and care-free days spent on writing the long-postponed novel fill our heads. But even success has its pitfalls. Here are a couple of potential problems to watch out for.

## PIGGY-BACKING

Should your book sell well enough for the publisher to offer you a contract on a second book, you could be tripped up by an insidious device called piggy-backing. Essentially, piggy-backing means that the advance for the second book will come out of the royalties from the first. Make sure your agent protects you against it. The publisher has to pay the advance, not you.

## "AUTHORITIS"

Be prepared for a change in attitude on the part of your client, who suddenly and happily has a literary reputation. By the time negotiations begin for a second book, "authors" are usually convinced they did write the first book that sounds so much like them.

Their perception of royalty percentages may also undergo a radical change, from pie in the sky to those lovely checks from the publisher in the mail twice a year. They may no longer like the idea of giving up 50%. Do not back down. It would be foolish and time-consuming for the author to end a successful relationship and go bargain-hunting for another writer.

## Perks

Every profession needs them, and those of celebrity ghosting can be especially nice.

### TRAVEL TO EXOTIC PLACES

I have taken my tape recorder to private tropical beaches, the better spas, and desert mountain tops—all those hideaways celebrities go to in order to have a little peace and quiet to "write" their books. Of course, I do not actually suggest that we go someplace luxurious. I describe the ideal book-collaborating conditions as monk-like, isolated, phoneless, faxless, devoid of all distractions of office and family. To the client this can translate into something like La Costa. Fine with me.

### BENEFITS TO FICTION WRITING

I live to write fiction, which may or may not be sold or even finished, although both are the goal and grand obsession. I find that ghost-writing is a valuable way to sensitize

my ear to a character's unique way of speaking. After several weeks of listening to the taped voice of my client and reading transcriptions, I begin to make seemingly unconscious word and style choices that are authentically the author's own. It is a joy to break out of the tyranny of one's own voice. Ghosting makes a writer keen to the nuances of speech—the word choices and sentence construction, the quirks and repetitions—and that developed sensitivity becomes a well-honed tool in fiction writing.

### THE "AUTHOR" DOES THE PROMOTING

While I roam around in the 1870s, developing the middle section of a novel, the author of my mini-bestseller is out on the radio-television-bookstore circuit, rushing from airport to airport, drinking weak coffee, promoting the book three and even four times a day. Me, I get to stay home—and that is the best part. Home is the book writer's natural habitat, and I have a few more months before I have to go scare up the next project.

# COLLABORATION AGREEMENTS: WHAT THEY SHOULD COVER

**Exclusivity**
: The collaborators agree to work with each other exclusively.

**Proposal**
: If you are doing all the writing, try to get paid for developing the proposal.

**Responsibility**
: The agreement should make it clear who will do what.

**Agents**
: Whether you have one agent or two, the relationship should be spelled out.

**Income**
: The financial arrangements have to be made as explicit as possible.

**Copyright**
: Make sure the copyright is registered in both your names.

**Bylines**
: Whose name comes first? *And* or *with*?

**Expenses**
: Clarify who will pay for expenses, especially in works that require a lot of illustrations or permissions.

**Term**
: It is common practice to make collaboration agreements co-extensive with the copyright of the book.

**Assignability**
: The contract should ensure that each party has the right to carry on with the work should his or her collaborator become unable to continue.

**Premature termination**
: Terms for termination of the contract should be spelled out.

**Arbitration**
: Should a disagreement arise, binding arbitration is a less expensive alternative to litigation.

# Agents

The role of the agent is much greater than just getting authors more money. At best, agents nurture writers, advocate for them, and act as buffers in the potentially hostile business environment of publishing.

In fact, agents are becoming more and more important in the publishing process. The NWU survey found that almost 80% of trade fiction books and 65% of trade nonfiction books were represented by an agent.

The increasing power that agents wield is both a blessing and a danger for writers. We have stronger allies in negotiating book deals, but it is also more difficult to approach publishers directly. And of course, we have to give up 15% (now more common than the traditional 10%) of our already inadequate writing incomes.

Having an agent to deal with the business side of writing also creates the temptation to wash one's hands of such matters. Needless to say, if you do not take an active interest in your own business, you open yourself up to disappointment and potential problems.

Agents can be great—especially ones who return your phone calls—but it is essential that writers be informed about such critical issues as contracts, rights, advances, and royalties.

## Agent Contracts

Traditionally, the relationship between authors and agents was only formalized in writing as a clause in a publishing contract. It is becoming much more common, however, for writers and agents to enter into separate written agreements. The points below summarize the key issues in such contracts. (They are based on the *NWU Preferred Literary Agent Agreement*, available to members.)

*See Membership Benefits, page 196.*

**B
O
O
K
S**

## SOME QUESTIONS TO ASK AN AGENT

**How much does she charge?**

Most agents now charge a commission of 15%, rather than the traditional 10%. The commission often does not cover mailing, copying, and telephone costs.

**Does he require a written contract?**

More and more do. Just make sure the contract is simple and that you are not under obligation for more than one book.

**Who are some of her clients?**

Have you heard of them and are they authors with your sensibilities? If the agent is reluctant to name clients, ask what well-known books she has sold. And you can easily obtain a partial client list by reading *Literary Agents of North America* or simply looking at the books in the office; many will be clients' books.

**How much does he like and understand your book?**

You'll glean this not only from the agent's enthusiasm, but by where he sees it being published, his ability to discuss the book intelligently, and how much he thinks it is worth.

**Will your book be auctioned or offered in multiple submission?**

If not, why not? Multiple submission may get you a bigger advance, but may not be right for your book.

**Does the agent have Hollywood connections?**

You never know what kind of project has film or TV potential.

## KEY ISSUES IN WRITER/AGENT CONTRACTS

- **Scope**—The contract should spell out precisely what you are hiring the agent to do.

- **Authority**—The contract has to give the agent the right to negotiate on your behalf but protect your ultimate decision-making power.

- **Compensation**—The financial arrangement should be detailed as clearly as possible.

- **Termination**—A procedure for ending the relationship has to be established.

- **Assignability**—Make sure that the agent cannot just pass you off to someone else without your permission.

- **Modification**—The contract should only be subject to modification in writing.

- **Arbitration**—Should a dispute arise, arbitration is the best alternative to litigation.

# Technical Writing: A User's Manual

Technical writing encompasses a plethora of sub-genres— from the writing of owners' manuals for toasters to the documentation of telecommunications switches to the development of environmental impact statements. Clearly, the skills and expertise required for each type of technical writing are different. Rates and working conditions, as you might expect, also differ depending on the kind of tech writing you do.

To talk sensibly about the economic conditions in technical writing, then, we need a convenient and logical way to subdivide the genre. One such way is by audience. In fact, there appear to be two distinct modes of technical writing—that for popular audiences (which we'll call "tech for the people") and that for expert audiences ("tech for techies"). Tech writing for popular audiences is any form of documentation designed for end users, the people who use a product, regardless of their level of technical expertise. Technical writing for expert audiences is the specialized communication of professional to professional. For example, the users' manual for a toilet on the space shuttle is tech for the people. A research report on the efficiency of the same toilet is tech for techies.

It is important to keep the distinction between the two types of technical writing in mind when evaluating prospects and contracts. The tech market is in the process of dividing economically. Pay rates for tech for the people are being driven down because so many people capable of writing "point-and-click" manuals are entering the field. Rates for people who have the technical skills to write tech for techies, on the other hand, are holding steady or rising.

## The Agency Debate

Depending on whom you talk to, technical service agencies, also known as jobbers or brokers, are either a necessary evil or an unnecessary evil. You might even find some technical writers who will say

T
E
C
H

W
R
I
T
I
N
G

that agencies are a godsend, but then again there are some people who think that a 286 computer is plenty fast enough. No matter: agencies are a fact of a technical writer's life.

So here is what you need to know about agencies: 1. Their profits come straight out of your pocket; and 2. You can get along without them.

*What you need to know about agencies: 1. Their profits come straight out of your pocket 2. You don't need them*

Agencies find writers for contracts that exist at client companies. The client does not pay directly for this service. If the agency succeeds in placing a writer, it bills the client for the writer's time, takes a cut, and pays the writer the remainder. Here is the tricky part: Even though the writer, in most cases, is directly responsible to the client for the quality of the work, it is the agency that determines how much the writer is paid.

There are innumerable stories of unethical agencies. In one anecdotal report, a jobber billed the client at $43 an hour and paid the writer on contract $18 an hour. That is a markup of close to 140 percent. Not bad, especially if the contract lasts several months or years.

Agencies can get away with such gouging because there are no established standards for rates in the tech market. It is your responsibility, therefore, to know what a fair rate is for specific types of work and to establish your own rate structure. Agencies have the right to make money on the services they provide to writers and clients (no more than 15 to 20 percent of the total billed to the client), but writers have to be in control of setting the wages for their labor.

*Rates &
Practices start
on page 123.*

Now, we have said that agencies are a fact of tech writers' lives. That is true; at one time or another in their careers most technical writers turn to agencies for contracts. Most established tech writers, however, prefer to work as independent contractors. In the NWU survey, for instance, more than 86 percent of responding technical writers described their careers as established or moderately established. Of the respondents, close to 70 percent rated their own marketing efforts and relationships with clients as the most productive sources of work, while 44 percent rated agencies as the least productive.

The obvious advantage of working as an independent is that you do not have to share your earnings with anyone. The drawback is that you have to hustle to get work. Then again, you are not likely to make a decent living without marketing yourself even if you work through agencies.

# Other Go-Betweens

*Contractors:* A contractor is anyone who agrees to provide technical writing services to a client and then subcontracts part or all of the work to other writers. Often, contractors are successful independent tech writers who have too much work.

Contractors are different from technical service agencies in that they remain responsible to the client for the quality and timeliness of the work. The contractor is usually actively involved in meeting with the client, commenting on content, and supervising and sometimes even training the subcontractor.

In general, contractors take 20 percent to 40 percent of the total billed to the client. But here, too, there are no established industry standards.

*Agents:* Agents, not to be confused with technical service agencies, are people who find work for tech writers but do not act as financial conduits. An agent will usually get the writer and the client together, provide some help in negotiating a contract, take a cut (generally 10 to 15 percent), and leave the stage. The writer is responsible to the client and bills the client directly.

*Documentation houses:* These are companies that contract with clients to produce documentation for their products. Documentation houses usually hire technical writers as permanent or temporary employees, pay them salaries, provide benefits, and withhold taxes.

In the rest of this chapter and in the next chapter, we will look at issues that concern all freelance technical writers, regardless of what type of tech writing they do or how they get their work.

# Contracts

Contracts are essential to a freelancer's economic well-being and mental health. Unfortunately, a great many freelance writers, including tech writers, overlook the importance of contracts. Many tech writers who would fearlessly and happily write a users' manual for a thermonuclear reactor seem to be intimidated by contracts. In our survey, the NWU found that only 46.5 percent of responding technical writers had written contracts for all of their projects and that on average the respondents had contracts for 63 percent of their work.

> *A contract is a piece of documentation, a manual for the relationship between the client and you*

A contract is nothing more than a piece of documentation. It is a manual, of sorts, for the relationship you and your client are entering. The clearer and simpler it is, the better it will do its job.

### FEES

Most technical writers charge by the hour; fewer charge per project. In the NWU survey, over 64 percent of tech writers indicated that their fees are hourly, and almost 25 percent said that they charge by the project.

If you are entering a contract with an hourly fee structure, it is important to state in writing how many hours a week you will work and whether overtime will be paid to you and at what rate. The duration of the contract is also important.

In a per-project contract, it is essential to specify the total number of hours that you will work and to spell out the financial arrangements in case that number is exceeded.

### PAYMENTS

NWU
RECOMMENDS

When you get paid is almost as important as how much you get. A client that pays you every two weeks at $40 an hour is easier to live with than one who pays $50 an hour, but only pays two months after each invoice. **Your contract should state clearly at what intervals you will bill the client and how long after each invoice you will receive payment.** (In the NWU survey, technical writers reported that on average they are paid three and a half weeks after billing.)

If you are going to work on a per-project-fee basis, the contract must specify the timing of payments. You should insist on getting some money up front. After that, payments should be made upon delivery of agreed-on portions of the project.

You can build penalties for late payments into your contracts, for example 10 percent for invoiced paid 30 days after invoice date. Conversely, you can make prompt payment more attractive by offering a discount—say 1 or 2 percent—for payment within 10 days of invoice.

## EXPENSES

Twenty-five percent of technical writers responding to the NWU survey said that their expenses are reimbursed either "rarely" or "never." This is a shocking statistic. It means that there are substantial numbers of writers out there who are actually paying part of their clients' costs of producing documentation. There is never any justification for your getting stuck with expenses (unless, of course, you are billing the client for the deluxe edition of the *Encyclopedia Britannica*, which you needed to look up the definition of *I/O switch*.)

**Contracts should clearly define what expenses will be reimbursed and whether there is a maximum amount.**

NWU
RECOMMENDS

T
E
C
H

## RIGHTS

The majority of technical writing contracts tends to be of the work-for-hire variety, where the copyright belongs to the client. In our survey, close to 63 percent of technical writers said that *all* of their contracts were work-for-hire, and on average over 73 percent of all respondents' contracts were of this type.

*See page 11 for an explanation of work for hire.*

W
R
I
T
I
N
G

In most cases, work-for-hire contracts are appropriate for technical writers, since if you are writing documentation you are in effect creating an extension of the client's intellectual property. If you are writing material that describes the product made by someone other than your client—a book about Microsoft Windows, let's say, that is being produced by a technical publisher—a work-for-hire contract is less justifiable, and you should be paid (handsomely) for signing over your rights to the client.

If the contract is not work-for-hire, it may contain an assignment-of-copyright clause. Make sure the clause stipulates that you sign over the copyright to the client only when all of your work has been paid for. This will give you leverage in settling accounts.

## REWRITES

As the old saying goes, there is no such thing as writing, there is only rewriting. Well, that is fine, as long as you get paid for it. This is especially true if you are getting paid on a per-project basis. It is imperative that the contract specify how many rewrites you will do. The contract should also spell out how much you will be paid for additional rewrites, over the number specified.

Although this may sound like a truism, many technical writers get burned on this point. In the NWU survey, 37 percent of respondents indicated that they do not get paid for additional rewrites.

Of course, if you are working on an hourly basis, the more rewrites the better.

## BYLINES

We have said that most technical writing is essentially an extension of the product it describes and therefore belongs to the client. The writer, however, should still get credit for his or her work. That is where bylines come in. The contract should specify how credit will be given on the published work.

If you cannot get your client to agree to give you an individual byline, organize your co-authors and demand bylines as a group.

## A FINAL WORD ABOUT CONTRACTS

Since technical writers tend to work for corporations, and quite often for huge corporations, most of your clients are likely to have a boilerplate contract. It is vital to remember two things about such contracts: (1) They are written with the client's, not your, interests in mind. (2) They are meant to be seen as starting points for negotiations, not as immutable pronouncements.

By their nature, boilerplates are designed to be changed. Negotiate. Cross out unfavorable terms. Write in your own conditions. Do whatever it takes to make the contract a good deal for you.

The same goes for purchase orders, which are increasingly replacing contracts in tech writing. Purchase orders serve the same purpose as contracts, spelling out the terms of the agreement between writer and client. Purchase orders are particularly likely to have boilerplate language inappropriate for a freelance writing project—e.g., payment 45 days after delivery of product or service. **Watch out for such boilerplate and modify it, using a letter of exception signed by the manager who is hiring you.**

**WARNING!**

# Technical Writing Rates & Practices

## A Word About the Numbers

This chapter will provide you with two kinds of information: A run-down of the rates and practices prevalent in the technical writing market to help you evaluate the deals you have been making; and NWU recommendations for acceptable rates and practices to help you make better deals in the future.

## Rates

Rates are given for six major classes of documentation, both for *tech for the people* (TP)—user's manuals for consumers; and for *tech for techies* (TT)—documentation for experts.

For each type of writing, four pieces of information about rates are provided: (1) the minimum and maximum reported hourly rates; (2) the average rate; (3) the prevalent range of rates in the market-place; and (4) the range of rates recommended by the NWU.

*(see chart on next page)*

**TECHNICAL WRITING: HOURLY RATES** ★

| | Min/Max | Average | Prevalent Range | NWU Recommends |
|---|---|---|---|---|
| **Hardware TP** | $16/50 | $35 | $25—50 | $30—50 |
| **Hardware TT** | $35/85 | $55 | $40—65 | $45—70 |
| **Software TP** | $10/45 | $30 | $20—35 | $30—50 |
| **Software TT** | $35/85 | $55 | $40—65 | $45—70 |
| **Biotech TP** | $18/50 | $30 | $20—40 | $30—50 |
| **Biotech TT** | $35/85 | $40 | $40—60 | $45—65 |
| **Medical Inst. TP** | $25/50 | $30 | $25—40 | $30—50 |
| **Medical Inst. TT** | $40/75 | $35 | $35—60 | $45—65 |
| **Corp. Procedures TP** | $10/50 | $30 | $20—40 | $25—40 |
| **Corp. Procedures TT** | $35/150 | $40 | $40—60 | $45—65 |
| **Defense TP** | $22/45 | $35 | $25—40 | $30—45 |
| **Defense TT** | $40/75 | $55 | $40—60 | $45—65 |

# Practices

## GETTING WORK

One of the most questionable pieces of lore in the technical writing marketplace is that to make it in tech writing you have to work through agencies. In our research, the NWU found that a large proportion of established tech writers do not use agencies.

We asked tech writers to rate several sources of work for effectiveness, based on how frequently they get projects from each source.

**SOURCES OF WORK**

| | Most effective | Effective | Somewhat effective | Not very effective | Not at all effective |
|---|---|---|---|---|---|
| **Writer's own marketing** | 44% | 19% | 10% | 15% | 12% |
| **Agencies** | 16% | 12% | 17% | 11% | 44% |
| **Business referrals** | 26% | 18% | 19% | 24% | 13% |
| **Friends** | 20% | 27% | 26% | 16% | 11% |
| **Job banks** | 12% | 14% | 30% | 11% | 43% |

Technical service agencies make profits by charging clients as much as possible and paying writers as little as possible. There might be times when you will have to work through an agency.

**Avoid service agencies when possible.**

## FEE STRUCTURE

We asked technical writers how they structure their fees: on an hourly, per-project, per-page, or other basis.

Given the complexity of many technical writing projects, it is often very difficult to estimate how much time you will need to complete a project. Unfortunately, most writers tend to underestimate and end up working much more and earning much less. In an hourly fee contract, you avoid having to pay a penalty if the project goes awry. Your clients are also less likely to drag their feet during the project if they are paying you by the hour.

| FEE STRUCTURE | (percentage of writers) |
|---|---|
| **Hourly** | 64% |
| **Per project** | 25% |
| **Per page** | 4% |
| **Other** | 8% |
| **NWU Recommends** ★ | hourly |

T
E
C
H

W
R
I
T
I
N
G

If you do charge on a per-project basis, try to build a maximum number of hours into the contract and a provision for renegotiating should the project go over that maximum.

## TIMELINESS OF PAYMENTS

We asked freelance technical writers how many weeks after invoice they get paid.

There is nothing as infuriating as working long hours on a project for which you have negotiated a good contract and not having enough money to pay the rent because the client takes months to pay your invoices. The way to protect yourself against this is to specify the terms of payment in the contract.

| TIMELINESS OF PAYMENTS | |
| --- | --- |
| Min/Max | 0/8 weeks |
| Average | 3—5 weeks |
| Prevalent range | 2—6 weeks |
| NWU Recommends | 2—4 weeks |

The ideal arrangement, obviously, is to be paid no later than 10 working days, or two weeks, after invoice. Try giving clients incentives in the form of discounts, for instance one or two percent.

Write in late-payment penalties—e.g., 10% for invoices paid later that 30 days after invoice date.

## EXPENSES

We asked technical writers how often their expenses are reimbursed by the client.

| EXPENSES REIMBURSED | | | |
| --- | --- | --- | --- |
| Never | 14% | Frequently | 14% |
| Rarely | 12% | Always | 37.5% |
| Sometimes | 22.5% | NWU Recommends | Expenses always reimbursed |

There is no justification for a writer to subsidize any part of a client's business. Make sure that your contracts stipulate that all reasonable expenses should be reimbursed. Specify the types of expenses considered reasonable and the maximum amount of reimbursement. It is also a good idea to have the client approve expenses before you lay out your own money.

## CONTRACTS

Signing on to a technical-writing project is the same as entering any business deal. The terms of the agreement have to be clearly spelled out before work begins or money exchanges hands. Many writers, however, still do not protect themselves by insisting on written contracts.

We asked technical writers for what percentage of their projects they have written contracts.

| **WRITTEN CONTRACTS** | |
| --- | --- |
| **Min/Max** | 0/99% |
| **Average** | 63% |
| **Prevalent range** | 50—99% |
| **NWU Recommends** ★ | Always have written contracts or purchase orders |

**WORK FOR HIRE**

In a follow-up question, we asked what proportion of projects with written contracts is work for hire. Not surprisingly, given the nature of technical writing, on average close to three-quarters of all tech-writing contracts are work for hire.

| | |
| --- | --- |
| **Min/Max** | 0/99% |
| **Average** | 73% |
| **Prevalent range** | 90—99% |
| **NWU Recommends** ★ | Work for hire is acceptable as long as you are certain that you cannot derive subsidiary income from the work. |

**BYLINES**

We have all certainly written our share of pieces we would rather not put our names to. However, if you are particularly proud of the manual you just wrote for a new auto-assembly robot, you have every right to a byline.

As the following statistics indicate, there is a tendency for tech writers not to get credit for their work.

| | |
|---|---|
| **Never** | 21% |
| **Rarely** | 27% |
| **Sometimes** | 27% |
| **Frequently** | 10% |
| **Always** | 15% |
| **NWU Recommends** ★ | Tech writers are entitled to bylines. |

## REWRITES

Rewriting, revising, getting it right—that is what writing is all about. Technical writers tell us that they generally rewrite pieces once or twice.

**REQUIRED REWRITES**

| | |
|---|---|
| **Min/Max** | 0/6 |
| **Average** | 1.5 |
| **Prevalent range** | 0—2 |
| **NWU Recommends** ★ | 0—2 times (for non-hourly contracts) |

---

**CONTRACTED REWRITES**

| | |
|---|---|
| Min/Max | 0/4 |
| Average | 1 |
| Prevalent range | 0—1 |
| NWU Recommends ✳ | 1—2 for non-hourly contracts. |

---

**ADDITIONAL REWRITES PAID FOR**

| | |
|---|---|
| Yes | 63% |
| No | 37% |
| NWU Recommends ✳ | Rewrites in addition to the number contracted for should be paid for, according to the terms of the contract. |

---

## TREATMENT

We asked technical writers whether they feel that they are treated in a professional, respectful, and fair manner by their clients. The answers were encouraging.

---

**WELL TREATED?**

| | |
|---|---|
| Yes | 90% |
| No | 10% |

---

# The Art of Survival

BY CHARLES THIESEN

I have noticed that most of the writers I know who pay all their bills with their writing have had pretty diverse careers. Like organisms surviving on the edge of a highly competitive ecology, we have to be bottom feeders—opportunists. The real success comes from surviving until you can make your living doing the writing you want to do most, most of the time.

For me at first, bottom-feeding opportunism meant accepting whatever writing job came along. When I started writing, I didn't know what it felt like to do the various kinds of writing jobs one could do—or even what many of those jobs were. I didn't know where to head, so I did whatever seemed doable. I wrote life-style pieces for magazines because I could get the assignments. I wrote a children's book about writing because I had taught writing to children. I had some medical background, so I did medical journalism; that led to writing pharmaceutical market reports. I just kept taking whatever jobs I could get that would pay me enough to keep writing.

After I had some credibility as a freelancer, bottom-feeding opportunism meant choosing between jobs. I wrote magazine articles rather than market reports because journalism sharpened my skills and was more interesting (even if it paid less). I switched to technical writing from magazine writing because it paid so much more that it gave me the flexibility to make other choices, as paid bills can.

The security of solid fees along with that flexibility wooed me away from other writing. I became predominantly a technical writer. After about six months I noticed that I was making a living. I had breathing space. I paused to consider where to go from there and realized that there was a kind of writing I wanted to do: novels.

This wasn't really a new desire. I had wanted to write a novel when I read Robert Heinlein's *Door Into Summer* as a teenager. I had wanted to write a novel when I read *Catch 22* in college. I had pushed this desire down beneath my view of reality, which said that writers were a kind of special talented people, and I was not.

But now that I had learned something about the craft of writing, I could think of writing a novel as a realistic ambition.

I started trying to carve out evening time for the novel and managed to work on it an average of, oh, five minutes a week. To be fair, four. Writing all day to pay the bills (along with car repair, doctors' appointments, clothes washing, and union activism) didn't leave much space for novelizing.

But being an opportunistic feeder had prepared me to apply leverage to my work life to make some of that space. For years, every decision I made about what job to try for and what job to take was made in the light of whatever I saw as my writing goal at that time. For about seven years, that writing goal had been little more than survival— earning as much of my living as possible by writing. Then earning as good a living as possible from my writing. Now I just had to add a new requirement: time for the novel.

About this time I got a contract to do software documentation. The client liked my work and before the contract was up, offered me a staff job. How could I seize the security of a job and still have freedom?

"If you guys like me so much," I said, "how about hiring me for a three-day week?" They agreed. They would pay me somewhat less than I made in my best freelance year. I would still pay for my own health insurance. And every week I would have four days for fiction.

In the past 16 months I've completed a bit more than half the novel. I write computer documentation 24 hours a week and suspense fiction 12 or so hours more. There isn't much overlap, but the discipline I've learned applies to both. So does a willingness to rewrite endlessly.

When I finish the novel, what happens to it is sure to affect my next series of opportunistic decisions. Maybe I'll get an advance for the next novel and add that to my salary so I can work more hours on fiction. Maybe the novel will disappear without a trace, I'll give up on novelizing, work full time and make some real money for a change. Maybe I'll have a blockbuster on my hands and move to Ireland.

There's not much doubt, though, that I'll keep on writing.

# Corporate / Nonprofit Communications Rates & Practices

## A Word About the Numbers

This chapter will provide you with two kinds of information: an overview of the rates and practices prevalent in the corporate and nonprofit communications markets, to help you evaluate the deals you have been making; and NWU recommendations for acceptable rates and practices, to help you make better deals in the future.

The information was gathered through the NWU survey and through interviews with union and nonunion writers, agents, and clients.

## Rates

The term corporate and nonprofit communications encompasses a broad range of writing, from ad copy and video scripts for large corporations to newsletters and press releases for grassroots nonprofits. We wanted to find out which types of projects are of particular importance to freelance writers and to determine the rates prevalent in the for-profit and nonprofit markets. With this in mind, we focused on seven major types of corporate and nonprofit writing: advertising copy, brochures, annual reports, newsletters, manuals, public relations materials, and scripts.

*(see chart on next page)*

For each type of writing, two sets of information are provided: (1) hourly rates for for-profit and nonprofit clients; and (2) the percentage of income respondents derived from corporate/nonprofit writing. Within each rate information set, the following statistics are provided: the minimum and maximum reported rates, the average rate, the range of rates prevalent in the marketplace, and the range of rates recommended by the NWU.

**HOURLY RATES**

| | | Min/Max | Average | Prevalent Range | NWU Recommends (at least) |
|---|---|---|---|---|---|
| **Ad Copy** | **For-profit** | $10/200 | $60 | $50—75 | $50—100 |
| | **Nonprofit** | $10/60 | $35 | $30—50 | $35—75 |
| **Brochures** | **For-profit** | $15/200 | $56 | $35—75 | $50—100 |
| | **Nonprofit** | $10/100 | $38 | $25—50 | $35—75 |
| **Annual Reports** | **For-profit** | $20/200 | $67 | $50—75 | $50—100 |
| | **Nonprofit** | $12/100 | $47 | $30—50 | $35—75 |
| **Newsletters** | **For-profit** | $8/250 | $58 | $50—75 | $50—100 |
| | **Nonprofit** | $10/100 | $38 | $25—50 | $35—75 |
| **Manuals** | **For-profit** | $15/75 | $50 | $40—75 | $50—100 |
| | **Nonprofit** | $5/65 | $35 | $30—50 | $35—75 |
| **Public Relations** | **For-profit** | $10/250 | $60 | $50—75 | $50—100 |
| | **Nonprofit** | $10/100 | $40 | $35—60 | $35—75 |
| **A/V Scripts** | **For-profit** | $10/250 | $65 | $50—75 | $50—100 |
| | **Nonprofit** | $10/100 | $37 | $30—50 | $35—75 |

**PERCENTAGE OF TOTAL INCOME DERIVED FROM CORPORATE/NONPROFIT WRITING**

| | % of income | | % of income |
|---|---|---|---|
| **Advertising Copy** | 5—10% | **Manuals** | 10—20% |
| **Brochures** | 5—20% | **Public Relations** | 5—20% |
| **Annual Reports** | 10—20% | **A/V Scripts** | 5—10% |
| **Newsletters** | 10—50% | | |

# *Practices*

**FEE STRUCTURE**

We asked corporate and nonprofit communications writers how they structure their fees, on an hourly.

| | percentage of respondents |
|---|---|
| **Hourly** | 47% |
| **Per project** | 43% |
| **Per page** | 2.5% |
| **Other** | 7.5% |
| **NWU Recommends** ✴ | Hourly |

We consider an hourly fee structure the most equitable and advantageous for freelance communications writers. It is often difficult to estimate how much time you will need to complete a project. Unfortunately, most writers tend to underestimate and end up working much more and earning much less. In an hourly fee contract, you avoid having to pay a penalty if the project takes longer than expected. Your clients are also less likely to drag their feet during the project if they are paying you by the hour.

If you do charge on a per-project basis, try to build a maximum number of hours into the contract and a provision for renegotiating should the project go over that maximum.

---

**TIMING OF PAYMENTS**

In freelance writing, getting a contract is often only half the battle; actually getting paid can be even more difficult. We asked freelance corporate and nonprofit communications writers how many weeks after invoice they get paid.

|  | Weeks after invoice |
|---|---|
| **Min/Max** | 0/15 |
| **Average** | 3.8 |
| **Prevalent range** | 2—6 |
| **NWU Recommends** | 2—4 |

---

There is no justification for payment delays of more than 30 days. The ideal arrangement, obviously, is to be paid no later than 10 working days, or two weeks, after invoice. To make this attractive to clients, you might consider offering a discount, say 2 on invoice total. You can build a penalty for late payments into your contracts—for instance, 10% for invoices paid 30 days after invoice date—to discourage clients from holding your money.

C
O
R
P
O
R
A
T
E
/
N
O
N
P
R
O
F
I
T

## REIMBURSEMENT OF EXPENSES

---

**HOW OFTEN ARE WRITERS' EXPENSES REIMBURSED BY THE CLIENT?**

| | |
|---|---|
| **Never** | 8% |
| **Rarely** | 6% |
| **Sometimes** | 15.5% |
| **Frequently** | 23% |
| **Always** | 48.5% |
| **NWU Recommends** ✴ | Expenses should always be reimbursed by the client. |

---

There is no justification for a writer to have to subsidize any part of his or her clients' business. All reasonable expenses should be reimbursed. Make sure that your contracts stipulate this and specify the types of expenses considered reasonable and the maximum amount of reimbursement. It is also a good idea to have the client approve expenses before you lay out your own money.

## CONTRACTS

Whether you are signing on to write a newsletter for your local soup kitchen or an annual report for a multinational pet-food conglomerate, you are entering a business deal. The terms of the agreement have to be clearly spelled out before work begins or money exchanges hands. Many writers, however, still do not protect themselves by insisting on written contracts.

---

**WRITTEN CONTRACTS**

| | |
|---|---|
| **Min/Max** | 0/99% |
| **Average** | 47% |
| **Prevalent range** | 0—50% |
| **NWU Recommends** ✴ | Always have a written contract |

---

CORPORATE / NONPROFIT

---

**WORK-FOR-HIRE CONTRACTS**

Close to 51 percent of respondents indicated that all of their contracts are work for hire. This is not surprising in light of the nature of corporate and nonprofit communications.

| | |
|---|---|
| **Min/Max** | 0/99% |
| **Average** | 63% |
| **Prevalent range** | 50—99% |
| **NWU Recommends** ✦ | Work for hire is acceptable as long as you are certain you cannot derive subsidiary income from the work. |

---

## BYLINES

As a corporate and nonprofit communications writer, you almost by definition have to remain in the background. You have every right, however, to receive credit for your work.

As the numbers below indicate, communications writers do not always get such credit.

---

**BYLINES RECEIVED**

| | |
|---|---|
| **Never** | 22% |
| **Rarely** | 21% |
| **Sometimes** | 24% |
| **Frequently** | 20% |
| **Always** | 13% |
| **NWU Recommends** ✦ | Byline on writer's request |

---

## REWRITES

| NUMBER OF REWRITES REQUIRED | |
|---|---|
| **Min/Max** | 0/6 |
| **Average** | 1.4 |
| **Prevalent range** | 0—3 |
| **NWU Recommends** ✸ | 0—2 (for non-hourly-fee contracts) |

| CONTRACTED REWRITES | |
|---|---|
| **Min/Max** | 0/3 |
| **Average** | 1.1 |
| **Prevalent range** | 0—2 |
| **NWU Recommends** ✸ | 1—2 (for non-hourly-fee contracts) |

| EXTRA REWRITES PAID FOR? | |
|---|---|
| **Yes** | 53.4% |
| **No** | 46.6% |
| **NWU Recommends** ✸ | Rewrites over the number specified in the contract should be paid for, according to the terms of the contract. |

## TREATMENT

We asked communications writers whether they feel that they are treated in a professional, respectful, and fair manner by their clients. The answers were encouraging.

| WELL TREATED? | |
|---|---|
| **Yes** | 90% |
| **No** | 10% |

# Where the Grass is Greener: Confessions of a Corporate Writer

BY KEITH WATSON

I knew there was a gap between what journalists and corporate writers earned, but I saw the division as a quaint creekbed. On one side of the gulch lived journalists, who wore cutoff jeans as they mowed crabgrass and pulled up pigweed. On the other side were corporate types, who wore stiff clothes, treasured suburbia, and paid others to mow their lawns. Since they supposedly had to suck up to people in business suits, I accepted that corporate writers should get higher pay.

After I left journalism and crossed over, I realized that the gap was not a mere gulch—it is a chasm. A steadily employed, freelance business writer can make five times what a freelance journalist earns in a year. And freelance business writers are treated with much greater respect. To show the disparities, here are some experiences from my career:

## JOURNALISM

I was asked to write a 3,500-word feature on personal finance for a city magazine. The offer of $1,750 didn't seem insulting. However, considering that I was asked to cover six complex areas—banking, brokerage, real estate, accounting, insurance, and legal services—the pay was meager. I took the assignment to "break in" at this magazine; instead, the magazine did its best to break me. After six weeks of researching, writing, and rewriting, the piece was accepted orally and then killed two weeks later. A typed note told me I would receive only $467.50 (not enough to pay my rent). At the same time, I was trying to collect on a four-month-old, overdue invoice from a Texas magazine. The editor had been fired and the business manager wasn't returning my calls.

## Business Writing

I was called in to write a 20-minute speech for a vice-president of marketing. I came in on a Tuesday morning and worked long hours for three intense days. On Friday morning, the executive delivered the speech and used only a few paragraphs of what I had written. But I billed the company $2,900 (rush rate) for my time and received the check within three weeks of invoice. The previous week, I had received a $4,200 check from a different firm for a 45-minute script I had written in about three weeks. The firm's managing partner also sent me a thank-you note.

So there you have it: less than $500 for six weeks of journalism work versus more than $7,000 for a month of commercial writing. The gap astounds and disgusts me. Education level and experience have virtually nothing to do with it. The gap is so wide that I don't know why any sane, experienced journalist beyond the age of 30 wouldn't cross the canyon and at least try doing commercial work. After all, magazines are running so many puff pieces and celebrity profiles that it's difficult to view the media as anything more than a commercial operation. In terms of content, the leap can be a mere hop, skip, and jump.

## Corporate Assignments

When freelance writers think of commercial writing, they usually think of ad copywriting, technical writing, and public relations. Many journalists fear becoming "flaks." But corporate America has many writing needs, most of which have little to do with media relations. The assignments can be arcane and dull, but I usually write about topics that challenge me, and I get an insider's view of business.

Perhaps I've been lucky, but none of my corporate clients—who might have been portrayed in my Vietnam War-era youth as evil, greedy titans—has stiffed me. Unlike the so-called "liberal media," which often lacks a sense of fair play, my clients don't understand the concept of a kill fee. My career switch may turn the stomachs of traditional union activists. But the media themselves, of course, are part of corporate America. And until journalists stop signing abusive contracts and working for peanuts, conditions in the publishing industry won't improve.

But back to the corporate market. Because of widespread layoffs ("downsizing" or "rightsizing," as these large-scale firings are called in press releases), an experienced journalist can make a good living as a freelance business writer. There's plenty of work—speeches, slide shows, video scripts, letters, ghost-written articles for trade journals—and the pay is often generous. But getting corporate work takes time, patience, and the right attitude. So here are some tips on making the transition:

### ASSEMBLE A PORTFOLIO

To get your foot in the door, examine what you've written and how your skills might translate in the business sector. If you've written feature stories, you could write profiles for internal newsletters or articles for corporate magazines distributed externally. If you've written about housing or architectural design, you could ask real estate firms if they need writing or editing help. But don't bring your poems or short stories to a marketing manager (unless he or she is a very good friend) and expect encouragement. Businesses aren't in business to subsidize your development as a creative writer.

### TO JUMP-START YOUR CAREER, MAKE COLD CALLS

After I had moved from Houston to Chicago, I could no longer rely on word-of-mouth to get assignments. Forced to get new work or starve, I decided to make cold calls. The first call was difficult, but they got much easier. I don't remember anyone being terribly rude (certainly not as rude as newspaper writers treat flaks). I suggest making five to 10 calls successively, which takes only an hour or less. Do all the calling at once so that your *spiel* becomes second-nature. Call marketing and public relations directors and ask, "I'm a freelance writer. Do you ever use freelancers?" If the answer is yes, send a résumé and writing samples. But don't expect instant call-backs. It may be a year before you receive a return call.

### HAVE FAITH

After you send out enough résumés, someone will call you—even if you lack solid credentials. For example, a public relations manager for a hospital chain espied my résumé and saw all the traveling I had done (Australia, Guatemala, Iceland, South Africa). She had lived abroad and wanted to meet me. Even though I had never done any health-care writing, she assigned me a piece about traveler's diarrhea for her hospital magazine. The idea was far from glamorous, but it was a fun piece to research and write. She liked it and assigned me quarterly pieces in her company's full-color magazine. She also asked me to write an occasional press release and ad copy. We became good friends and, with that work, I was able to get other corporate assignments.

### Care About Your Clients

Many writers hope to make a quick buck off corporations so they can go home and write fiction. I have no problem with doing commercial work to support your serious writing. But I don't think you can succeed as a business writer unless you honestly care about helping clients with their writing needs. If you think of the work as "easy money," your attitude is going to show and you won't get repeat business.

### Do Pro-Bono Work

A good number of corporate folks, unfortunately, lack imagination and fear the slightest risk. For example, if there isn't a press release in your portfolio, some people will assume that you're incapable of writing one. Never mind that you might have seen tens of thousands of releases and you could write them in your sleep. They need to hold one of yours in their hands. So, if you need to beef up your portfolio, do some pro-bono press releases or a brochure for a charity. But make sure your volunteer work looks good. For example, I wrote an annual report for a public television station that won a national award from PBS. That gorgeously photographed and designed report earned me zero but helped me get a lucrative assignment to write an annual report for a law firm.

### Mind Your Manners

Civility is a treasured value in corporate America, and a marketing director doesn't want to take a chance on an unknown writer being less than kind to the higher-ups. Of course, there are dress codes as well. A bearded, long-haired fiction writer once asked me how he could get "some of that high-paying corporate work." Well, let's face facts: unless you're a respected creative director at an ad agency, you won't get away with exposed tattoos, multiple body piercings, and long stringy hair. The upside of the corporate dress codes is that, particularly for men, dressing dull can be cheaper than dressing hip. I found a great used-clothing store in Chicago that stocked boring men's suits for $25 each. I have bought standard-issue black wingtips for $80 and less. I refuse to pay good money for clothing that I don't want to wear. Once I started making money, I bought a couple of suits on sale for $300 each.

### Consider a Full-Time Position

If you desperately need steady income, I would recommend

pursuing a full-time job in a marketing communications department. After my $467.50 debacle with the city magazine, I started looking for freelance corporate work but was asked by one firm to apply full time. Considering my years of experience, the salary offer was mediocre. I took the job, however, to learn the corporate ropes and get a steady paycheck. After a year and a half, I left the firm on good terms and took a good deal of freelance work with me. Oddly enough, the company was happy to pay me four times an hour what they had paid me to be on staff. Corporations tend to take for granted in-house writers, whom they rarely promote, so it's better to be freelance.

As a child of the '60s, I never thought I'd "go corporate." But I got tired of editors passing up my story ideas, such as churches' slow response to the AIDS crisis or the seamy side of standup comedy shops. They wanted upbeat, non-controversial pieces that created a cozy editorial environment to satisfy advertisers and intoxicate readers into consuming more, more, more. So, instead of doing meaningful articles with an iconoclastic bent, I found myself writing "service pieces" about how to choose a plastic surgeon and "advertorials" about

real-estate developments. I didn't become a journalist for this.

I would never advise young writers, however, to pass up journalism in favor of high-paying work. When you're in your 20s and single, who needs money? I am, in fact, puzzled by college students who aspire to work for a buttoned-down corporation. No one learns how to write well inside a big business.

The tragedy of the vast pay gap between journalists and corporate writers is that the quality of journalism suffers as mature writers leave the field. The quality has already declined because the industry loves to hire interns from wealthy families and freelancers with support from a spouse. Thus, the articles are written by and geared toward upper-income readers.

I will occasionally write a magazine article for an editor-friend if no kill fee is involved, if payment is timely, and if the assignment interests me. But I no longer allow my labor to subsidize the production of profit-making magazines. Because of my switch to corporate work, I'm able—at age 40—to save for retirement and think about buying a home. Sad to say, but these fundamentals of the American dream are beyond the reach of nearly all freelance journalists.

# Literary Magazines
# Rates & Practices

Literary magazines, or small-press magazines as they are sometimes called, comprise the major market for poetry and fiction. There are thousands of these publications, from well-established reviews published by universities to tiny magazines published by individuals on their home computers. Although most of these publications have rather limited circulations, as a group they give poets and fiction writers access to a large audience and the all-important opportunity for exposure.

As a group, literary magazines present writers with particular problems. In the following sections, we will look at the practices and working conditions prevalent in the literary magazine market.

## Rates

You probably did not go into writing poetry or fiction for the money. In fact, writers seriously committed to making it in these genres must be prepared to support themselves by other means.

When asked how often they get paid for work published by literary magazines, for instance, participants in the NWU survey answered as follows:

| FREQUENCY OF PAY | |
| --- | --- |
| Never | 25% |
| Rarely | 31% |
| Sometimes | 25% |
| Frequently | 6% |
| Always | 13% |

As you can see, the chances of getting paid by literary magazines are slim. This does not mean, however, that these publications do not pay as a rule or that they should not be expected to pay. Here, a distinction has be made between the well-established publications and the truly "little" magazines.

Publications such as *American Short Fiction, Descant, New England Review, Ploughshares, Poetry, The Southern Review,* and others like them are supported by universities or foundations. They, therefore, do not rely on sales to cover their operating costs and usually make an attempt to pay writers. Below are the rates paid by these publications for poetry, short fiction, critical essays, and reviews. For each genre, four pieces of information are presented: (1) the minimum and maximum reported rates; (2) the average rate; (3) the range of rates prevalent in the marketplace; and (4) range of rates recommended by the NWU.

**LITERARY MAGAZINE RATES**

| | Min/Max | Average | Prevalent Range | NWU Recommends (at least) |
|---|---|---|---|---|
| **Poetry** | $0/100 | $15 | $0—25 | $10—30 |
| **Short Fiction** | $0/800 | $66 | $0—50 | $25—100 |
| **Criticism** | $0/500 | $84 | $0—100 | $25—150 |
| **Reviews** | $0/500 | $79 | $0—200 | $25—200 |

Research the market before you submit work to literary magazines and demand to be paid by well-established publications.

## Payments

A problem that all freelance writers often run into is that publishers take a long time to pay. When a publisher holds on to money owed to you for months, he or she is essentially forcing you to provide an interest-free loan. There is no justification for this practice. Writers have to demand to be paid promptly.

For writers who publish in literary magazines this is both more and less of a problem than for other writers. Since the amounts of money involved tend to be nominal, it is doubtful that you would be waiting for the check to arrive so you can pay your rent. On the other hand, you are unlikely to see any money at all for over a year after publication, since literary magazines as a rule pay on publication—on average, six months after acceptance, which in turn usually takes place about four months after you submit the work for consideration. To make matters worse, it is common for magazines to delay payment after publication.

| PAYMENT DELAY AFTER PUBLICATION (IN MONTHS) | |
| --- | --- |
| Min/max | 0/16 |
| Average | 2.3 |
| Prevalent range | 1—3 |
| NWU Recommends ✴ | Payment within 30 days of acceptance |

No matter how insignificant the amount is to your survival, a year is too long to wait to get paid for work that has been published. If the magazine is interested in your writing, the editors should make a commitment to publish it and pay you within 30 days of accepting the work.

## Free Copies

Unfortunately, payment in cash tends to be the exception in the world of literary magazines. The common practice is to pay writers in free copies of the issues in which their works appear. Some magazines, however, will not even offer this small token.

L
I
T
E
R
A
R
Y

| NUMBER OF CONTRIBUTOR'S COPIES | |
|---|---|
| Min/Max | 0/15 |
| Average | 2.8 |
| Prevalent Range | 1—3 |
| NWU Recommends | 2—6 |

At minimum, you should receive two free copies of the issue in which your work appears, regardless of whether you have been paid for the work or not.

## Submissions

| RESPONSE TIME | |
|---|---|
| One of the major complaints voiced by writers who publish in literary magazines is the inordinately long time publishers take to respond to submissions. | |
| | Months |
| Min/Max | 0/12 |
| Average | 3.6 |
| Prevalent Range | 1—6 |
| NWU Recommends | 1—3 months |

The majority of literary magazines work with skeletal or nonexistent staffs. It is understandable, therefore, that they need time to respond to submissions. There is no justification, however, for a publisher to take longer than three months to respond.

**MULTIPLE SUBMISSIONS**

Given the length of time it takes literary magazines to respond to submissions, it is a good idea to send your work to more than one publication at a time. That's one argument. The other says: It is best to carefully research your market and send to the magazines most likely to accept your work, one at a time.

We asked literary-magazine contributors how often they submit to more than one publication simultaneously.

| | |
|---|---|
| **Never** | 33% |
| **Rarely** | 13% |
| **Sometimes** | 26% |
| **Frequently** | 17% |
| **Always** | 11% |
| **NWU Recommends** ★ | Provided the magazines to which you are submitting do not have a policy against the practice, multiple submissions are likely to improve your chances of having your work published. |

# *Publication*

Waiting for a response to your submission is only the beginning. After your work is accepted, you will have to wait even longer to see it in print. The problem, in part, is that most literary magazines are published quarterly, semiannually, or even annually.

| **TIME OF PUBLICATION (IN MONTHS AFTER ACCEPTANCE)** | |
|---|---|
| **Min/Max** | 0/21 |
| **Average** | 6.1 |
| **Prevalent Range** | 2—12 |
| **NWU Recommends** ★ | Publication within one year of acceptance |

L
I
T
E
R
A
R
Y

Although there are constraints within which literary magazines have to work, they should make every effort to notify the author of the projected publication date—within one year of final acceptance. If the date is unacceptable, the author has the right to withdraw the work and submit it to other publications.

# Copyright

In submitting your work for publication, whether paid or unpaid, you are offering the publisher a limited grant of rights to publish the work, usually first North American print rights. Some publishers, however, try to gain control of the copyright to the work. This practice is unacceptable.

Copyright is your claim to ownership of the work and the assurance of your continued ability to reproduce the work and to derive income from it. Once you sign over the copyright to a publisher, you have to get the publisher's permission to reprint the work or use it in any other way.

We asked poets and fiction writers how often they retain copyright of their published work.

**WARNING!**
**Do not sign over your copyright**

| RETAINING COPYRIGHT | |
|---|---|
| **Never** | 7% |
| **Rarely** | 4% |
| **Sometimes** | 8% |
| **Frequently** | 20% |
| **Always** | 61% |

These numbers are discouraging. Authors are signing over their copyrights in significant numbers. You get paid little enough, if at all. At least make sure that you can publish your work again without having to get someone else's permission.

LITERARY

## *Treatment*

We have talked about the problems writers encounter in dealing with literary magazines. But how do poets and fiction writers feel about the way they are treated by these publications?

We asked writers whether they feel that they are treated professionally, fairly, and respectfully by the editors and staff of small press magazines.

| WELL TREATED? | |
| --- | --- |
| **Yes** | 77% |
| **No** | 23% |

Literature, readers, writers, and the publishers themselves would benefit if more writers received better treatment from literary magazines. We believe that the recommendations we have made in this chapter would go a long way to improving the situation.

L
I
T
E
R
A
R
Y

# Feeding the Spirit: A Poet's Perspective on Writing for Literary Magazines

BY ALEX HALBERTSADT

If you write poetry, you almost certainly know something about the way poetry is published and read in the United States. Which is to say that you are familiar with the literary journal—the forum and marketplace of poetry in this country since the times of Stevens, Williams, and Eliot. And if you are like most poets who submit work to these publications, you probably feel a certain amount of ambivalence toward them.

My initial encounter with the contemporary published poem was, like that of many readers, in the venerable dinosaurs of literary journals—*Anteus*, *The Paris Review*, *Grand Street*, and other glossy, expensively produced magazines that publish established authors with national and often international reputations. On the other side of the spectrum were the stapled, mimeographed "booklets" that felt like, and often were, published by a single person hunched over a computer in the privacy of his or her own bedroom. Some of these magazines were local, others eccentric, many quite good. On the whole, literary journals seemed to be repositories of technique—alluring, even lofty. And almost every one of them welcomed submissions (although some less actively than others).

But in the process of actually submitting poems, the journal, and the field of poetry as a whole, became defined to me by its limitations and often bizarre rituals. As my writer friends were trying to sell articles to *Esquire* or reviews to *Spin*, I was sending my poems to magazines with names like *Talisman* and *Asylum Annual*, which had circulations that were small fractions of those of the glossies and could often only be found in university libraries or specialty bookstores. And in response, I was getting everything from multipage contracts in triplicate to comments scrawled directly on the self-addressed, stamped envelopes I dutifully enclosed. At times, I received no response at all.

I found that some of my favorite literary magazines were read exclusively by other poets and were unknown to almost everyone else. A recent survey, in fact, showed that more than three-quarters of the people who read literary journals are themselves writers.

When I did publish poems, I rarely received any money for them. The common payment at even the most successful journals is two contributor's copies. And I have often received less than that.

Those magazines that do pay usually remit sums that generally cannot cover the cost of a pizza. In today's literary climate, it often seems as though having a poetry manuscript accepted by a journal is considered a privilege rather than a product of diligent, compensable labor. When a well-known, West Coast literary journal recently paid me $50, seven contributor's copies, and, yes, a 100 percent-cotton t-shirt for a long poem, I was amazed at my good fortune. It was a windfall by poetry standards, and I was torn between extreme gratitude to a magazine that pays more than it can get away with, and cynicism about the paltry economic value of creative writing in this society.

In a sense, the notion of being a "professional poet" is somewhat of an oxymoron. Last year, I spent more money on postage, laser prints, and copies than I made from my published poems. I suspect the same is true of many in the poetry business. The career track appears equally monastic—the number of individuals in this country who are making a living exclusively from their poetry can be counted on the fingers of one hand.

This tradition goes back to Wallace Stevens' office at the Hartford Accident & Indemnity Company, where he dictated poems to his secretary, and to Paterson, New Jersey, where Dr. W.C. Williams scribbled poems on prescription pads between treating sprained ankles and common colds.

Today, being a poet means having a job, even for the most prolific and the best selling. The luckier ones support themselves by writing in other genres, editing, or teaching. Journals, by the way, are rarely profitable either—many rely on university patronage and grants, as well as on the efforts of grossly underpaid editors—a fact that often explains the nominal sums received by their contributors.

A poet's more mundane struggles are those experienced by most freelance writers: the rolls of stamps, the endless copying of manuscripts, the seemingly eternal waiting, and, of course, the fierce competition. Most of the better journals receive thousands of manuscripts annually and accept only one to three percent of the submissions. The common prohibition against simultaneous submissions means that one has to wait up to several months for a response before being able to resubmit a manuscript to another journal.

Ultimately, poetry is an art, a personal matter. For me, the challenges and pleasures reside in the cultivation of form, the increasing pliability of language. And literary journals offer the opportunity to experiment and to share the work with an audience.

The small, specialized audiences of literary magazines are to some extent blessings in disguise. Those who spend their time reading poetry usually know and care about it to an exceptional degree. It is precisely this devoted, tenacious community of readers that makes publication in even the humblest journal so rewarding: You are assured of a careful reading and the appreciation of the effort. This makes the hardships of a professional poet's life a little easier to bear.

# Publish & Perish

Some people might wonder why a book on freelance writing includes a section on academics. True, many academic do not see writing as their primary professional pursuit or identity, nor certainly as a major income source. But it is also true that academics produce a large proportion of all published writing and that publishing is crucial for most academic careers. And precisely because writing is not explicitly part of an academic's job, these writers are, in fact, freelance.

## The Need to Publish

It is a fact of academic life that to succeed you have to publish. At every stage of an academic career, one's productivity as an author is an important gauge. Whether you are looking for a first job, trying to change jobs, being reviewed for tenure, or are up for a salary increase, your publication list plays a critical role.

This "publish-or-perish" climate makes academic writers particularly vulnerable to inequitable treatment by publishers. Since an academic's livelihood depends on his or her ability to publish, most academic writers would choose to accept an unfair publishing deal rather than run the risk of alienating the publisher by negotiation for better conditions.

*Worried about alienating publishers, academics often accept unfair deals*

Can this be changed? The National Writers Union believes it can. By arming ourselves with information and standing up for our rights, all writers, including academics, can begin to develop consistent, equitable standards in publishing.

The sections that follow deal with some of the issues of particular importance to academic writers.

# Copyright

The most insidious trend in academic publishing is the seizure of copyright. Both book publishers and academic journals frequently pressure authors to sign over the copyright to the publisher.

A typical grab for copyright on the part of a publisher is likely to be worded something like:

> *The Press requests your permission to copyright your work in the name of the Press. This does not mean that the Press owns the material, but simply that the copyright is in the Press's name. We ask you to grant the Press the full and exclusive right during the term of the copyright to publish or allow others to publish your contribution in all forms and in all languages throughout the world.*

**WARNING!**

**This is an expert piece of obfuscation, or to put it more bluntly, a con job. What the language in these two paragraphs is trying to do is to blur the distinction between copyright and publishing rights.**

Copyright ensures the author of a work the legal ownership of that work. It is patently untrue, therefore, to say that the holder of the copyright does not own the copyrighted material.

*See page 7 for a discussion of copyright.*

Publishing rights are the conditions under which the copyright holder authorizes the publisher to print and sell the work. By including a grant of publishing rights, the publisher in the above example is attempting to reinforce the impression that the author would remain the owner of the work after signing the copyright over to the publisher. This is simply not true, and the second clause is irrelevant.

To pacify authors, a publisher trying to seize the copyright will often include in the contract a clause such as this:

> *The Author may publish his/her work after informing the Press of the planned publication. No payment will be required, but reference should be given to the original publication.*

In other words, you will essentially have to get the publisher's permission to reprint your work in the future. You will not, however, have to pay for it. Surprisingly, many academic writers are taken in by this "generosity" on the part of publishers.

ACADEMIC

Publishers are not the only ones guilty of taking advantage of academic writers' need to publish by seizing their copyrights. Some colleges and universities require their faculties to register copyright of published work in the name of the institution. The rationale for this is that the work was produced while the author was an employee of the college/university, and therefore, belongs to the institution.

*Some colleges now require faculty members to register copyright of all their work in the institution's name*

The seizure of copyright—by publisher and colleges and universities—is an exploitative practice, for which there is no justification. It subverts the principles on which U.S. copyright law is founded, and it robs writers of the products of their intellectual labors.

**Beware of copyright clauses in your contracts and negotiate hard to retain your copyright.**

WARNING!

## Contracts

A surprisingly high proportion of academic writers enter into agreements with publishers without a written contract. In our research, for instance, we found that close to 54 percent of academics never have written contracts with the professional journals in which they publish.

There is no reason not to have a contract with your publisher. Contracts define relationships. And should disagreements arise, they make it easier to sort things out.

In considering contracts, it is vital to remember that they are written with the publisher's—not your—interests in mind, and that they are meant to be seen as starting points for negotiations, not take-it-or-leave-it propositions.

**Just about all contracts are in large part boilerplates. By their nature, boilerplates are designed to be changed. You should never, therefore, just sign. Negotiate.**

WARNING!

A
C
A
D
E
M
I
C

# Payments

Another way in which the "publish-or-perish" mentality affects academic writers is the level of financial remuneration they receive for published work. Put simply, academic writers tend to get the short end of the stick because publishers know that academics are likely to accept any conditions as long as their work is printed.

To give an example from our research, the average advance for trade nonfiction is a little over $20,000; the Authors Guild found that the median was around $20,000. Meanwhile, academic writers in our survey reported the average advance for college texts to be about $5,300. This discrepancy is obviously not based on the amount of work that goes into the writing of the respective books, potential sales, or profit margins. The most probable explanation is that academic writers are more likely to accept lower advances.

The situation is even more troubling if one looks at professional journals. Not only is it practically unheard of for journals to pay authors, a significant proportion actually charge writers review and production fees. And some go as far as to charge submission fees. In case you are not familiar with this practice, a submission fee is the money you pay a journal simply to consider your article for publication.

# Free Speech

All writers have to deal with the issue of censorship, even if it is not overt. Publishers' editorial policies essentially determine what opinions will and will not be heard.

*More on censorship, page 173.*

This problem is compounded for academic writers by their accountability to the institutions for which they work. In the past several years alone, we have witnessed a number of heated debates over the limits of free speech in academia.

No one has the right to dictate what authors can and can not write. The National Writers Union holds that it is our responsibility to work against all forms of censorship.

# Academic Writing Rates & Practices

Books and professional journals are the primary outlets for academic writers. These two markets, although equally important, are very different in the kinds of issues they present.

Although book publishers often treat academic writers somewhat differently from other authors, the basic economic and contractual issues involved are the same for all book authors. This guide's section on book writing provides information on all the critical aspects of book publishing—contracts, rates and practices, and agents—to help you evaluate your book deals.

In the following discussion, we will look at the practices and conditions prevalent in the academic-journal market, which is the exclusive province of scholarly writers, and which possesses unique characteristics and poses special problems. Along with findings from our research, we will present NWU's recommendations for minimum standards.

*More on book writing: page 67.*

## Academic Journals: Who Needs Them?

We wanted to find out just how deeply ingrained the "publish-or-perish" principle is in academic writers' psyches and what role academic journals play in this scheme of things. We therefore asked writers how important the ability to publish in the academic press is to their professional success

*(see chart on next page)*

A
C
A
D
E
M
I
C

| IMPORTANCE OF ABILITY TO PUBLISH TO CAREER | |
|---|---|
| **Extremely Important** | 30.1% |
| **Very Important** | 17.5% |
| **Important** | 14.7% |
| **Somewhat Important** | 20.3% |
| **Not at All Important** | 17.4% |

It is important to note that almost 80 percent of the academic writers who participated in our research described their careers as established or moderately established.

## Getting Paid or Paying?

Pay rates are not an issue for most academic writers for the simple reason that most academic journals do not pay. We asked writers how often they get paid by academic journals and found the following.

| ACADEMIC JOURNALS PAY | |
|---|---|
| **Never** | 60.3% |
| **Rarely** | 25.5% |
| **Sometimes** | 5% |
| **Frequently** | 2.8% |
| **Always** | 6.4% |

It is not surprising, then, that almost 50 percent of academic writers we talked to reported that their annual writing income was below $2,000.

## CONTRIBUTOR'S COPIES

The only payment most academic writers get are free copies of the issue of the journal in which their work appears. Even here, however, the treatment writers receive varies greatly.

| | |
|---|---|
| **Min/Max reported** | 0/50 |
| **Average** | 6 |
| **Prevalent range** | 1—5 |
| **NWU Recommends** ✸ | No less than 5 |

In addition to free copies of the whole issue, you can usually get a fair number of reprints of your article. As many as the first 20 to 50 are free.

## READER'S OR REVIEW FEES CHARGED

Not only do academic writers not get paid for published work, some journals charge reader's or review fees as a condition of publication.

| | |
|---|---|
| **Always** | 1% |
| **Frequently** | 2.5% |
| **Sometimes** | 6% |
| **Rarely** | 10.5% |
| **Never** | 80% |
| **NWU Recommends** ✸ | No review fees |

A
C
A
D
E
M
I
C

It is bad enough that academic writers basically have to donate their articles to have them published. It is unconscionable for academic journals to require writers to subsidize the publication of their own work.

## *Contracts*

"Why do I need a contract," some academics might say, "if there is no money involved?" In fact, our research showed that the majority of academics do not have written contracts with the journals that publish their work.

---

**WRITERS HAVE CONTRACTS WITH ACADEMIC JOURNALS**

| | |
|---|---|
| **Never** | 53.9% |
| **Rarely** | 21.5% |
| **Sometimes** | 12.3% |
| **Frequently** | 3.1% |
| **Always** | 9.2% |
| **NWU Recommends** | Always have a written contract |

---

Contracts are important for a variety of reasons, the key being the rights you are granting to the publisher. Even if you are not being paid for your work, the contract spells out the legal and professional foundations of the relationship between you and the publisher. Contracts also make it easier to settle disputes, should they arise.

# *Rights*

## COPYRIGHT OWNERSHIP

The question of rights is one of the most serious issues in academic publishing. There is a major trend among publishers of academic journals—and to a lesser extent among colleges and universities—to require academic writers to register the copyrights to their works in the name of the publisher or the college or university.

In our research we found that academic writers retain copyright of their published work with the following frequency.

| RETAINING COPYRIGHT | |
|---|---|
| **Always** | 27.2% |
| **Frequently** | 18% |
| **Sometimes** | 18% |
| **Rarely** | 18% |
| **Never** | 18.8% |
| **NWU Recommends** | Always retain copyright |

**WHO HAS THE COPYRIGHT?**

We asked academic writers in whose name copyright of published work is registered in cases where they do not retain it.

| | |
|---|---|
| **Publisher** | 80.5% |
| **College/University** | 16% |
| **Other** | 3.5% |

It would be an understatement to say that these statistics are alarming. Your copyright is your claim to authorship—and thus ownership. By registering copyright in someone else's name, you essentially give up ownership of your work.

Contracts should grant the journal publishing rights of a specified geographic scope, for a specified time period. The publishing rights traditionally purchased by trade magazines, for example, are first North American print publication rights. Do not confuse copyright and publishing rights.

*For details on rights, see page 7.*

A
C
A
D
E
M
I
C

# *Waiting*

A common complaint among academics is the amount of time it takes publications to respond to submitted material and then to publish work they accept. Academic writers are certainly not alone in this. Journalists, poets, and book authors have similar problems and express the same frustration. Given the importance publication is to an academic's career, it is easy to understand the concern.

---

**RESPONSE TO SUBMISSIONS**

The days after sending an article to a publication for review can be the longest in one's life. Will it be judged to be well researched and written? Is it significant enough? Is it original? Under such emotional pressure, a week can seem an eternity. And it usually takes publications a lot longer than a week to respond to submitted articles.

We found the following conditions among academic journals:

|  | Months |
|---|---|
| **Min/Max reported** | 0/41 |
| **Average** | 5.4 |
| **Prevalent range** | 2—6 |
| **NWU Recommends** ★ | 2—3 months |

---

Even after your article has been accepted, you are not really home free. Many publications have long backlogs of material and therefore take months to print articles. This becomes more of a problem because some colleges and universities do not recognize a publication credit until the work actually appears in print.

| TIME OF PUBLICATION | |
| --- | --- |
| | Months After Acceptance |
| **Min/Max** | 0/30 |
| **Average** | 10 |
| **Prevalent range** | 3—12 |
| **NWU Recommends** ✦ | 2—6 months |

## *Simultaneous Submission*

When asked about submitting articles to more than one journal at the same time, one academic writer answered succinctly: "Major sin." Journals either strongly discourage or prohibit the practice outright.

There are even stories of academics who have been censured by their colleges or universities for using multiple submissions.

None of this, however, seems to have discouraged all academics. In the course of our research we asked academic writers how often they submit work to more than one publication at the same time.

| FREQUENCY OF MULTIPLE SUBMISSIONS | |
| --- | --- |
| **Never** | 66.7% |
| **Rarely** | 15.9% |
| **Sometimes** | 10.3% |
| **Frequently** | 5.6% |
| **Always** | 1.5% |

A
C
A
D
E
M
I
C

## *Treatment*

We have talked about the problems that confront academic writers on their quests to publish in professional journals. But how do academics feel about the treatment they receive at the hands of the people who run these publications?

We asked writers whether they feel that they are treated professionally, fairly, and respectfully by the editors and staff of academic journals. The rather depressing results:

| WELL TREATED? | |
| --- | --- |
| Yes | 77% |
| No | 23% |

The NWU believes that academic writers should receive equal, fair treatment from publishers. It is up to each writer to arm him- or herself with information and to demand equitable contracts and working conditions. The union can help in this effort.

A
C
A
D
E
M
I
C

*The Politics of Writing*

# Censorship

BY ROBERT B. CHATELLE

*"Censorship is the strongest drive in human nature; sex is a weak second."*
—Journalist Phil Kerby, quoted in Nat Hentoff's *Free Speech for Me—But Not for Thee*

One who's never felt the urge to censor doesn't care very much about anything or anybody. I wouldn't pick such a person for a friend. But the urge to censor must always be resisted. Oppression depends upon ignorance, and oppressors maintain power by damming the flow of information. Censorship is spiritual violence—the ultimate evil because it obstructs thought and imprisons the spirit.

The clearest definition of censorship comes from Marjorie Heins, ACLU Arts Censorship Project Director: "Censorship is anything that reduces the availability of free expression. If something has the intention or effect of limiting what can be seen or heard, it's censorship." Government censorship is proscribed by the First Amendment. But since the First Amendment is government interpreted and enforced, it historically has provided us scant protection. Whenever the state wishes to censor, the Supreme Court can usually be counted on to create a convenient new "exception." Occasionally, a free-expression advocate—such as William O. Douglas—achieves the bench. But by and large, the Judiciary is as hostile to free expression as the rest of government. Most current censorship, however, is effected not directly by government but rather by private citizens and organizations—pro-censorship groups, such as the Reverend Donald Wildmon's American Family Association, and by media owners and advertisers.

**Censorship is spiritual violence: It obstructs thought**

The argument for censorship is seductively compelling: (1) speech is powerful; (2) anything powerful is dangerous; (3) anything dangerous should be regulated; (4) therefore, speech should be regulated.

People on the Left and the Right often disagree about *which* speech should be regulated—they consider speech dangerous for differing, though overlapping, reasons. Right-wingers believe that free speech is not only sinful in itself but that it *causes* sin—i.e., sexual behavior that meets their disapproval. Left-wingers believe that free speech "constructs" inequality. And both Right and Left buy the fallacious notion that some speech is so powerful that it overwhelms free will and actually *causes* violence.

## Attacks on the NEA

In recent years, the most-reported right-wing censorship campaigns have been directed against the National Endowment for the Arts (NEA), especially attacks on two visual artists: Andrés Serrano and Robert Mapplethorpe. Many writers are unaware that other important NEA attacks have targeted writers. The first right-wing attack occurred in 1969, when Congressman William Scherle (R-IA) railed against Aram Saroyan's poem "LIGHGHT," which appeared in the NEA-sponsored *American Literary Anthology/2*. Because of this controversy, Nixon-appointed NEA Chair Nancy Hanks intercepted the *American Literary Anthology/3* galleys and demanded that a story be deleted. When editor George Plimpton refused, Hanks canceled funding and terminated the entire series. In 1972, freshman Senator Jesse Helms (R-NC) launched his first NEA attack when NWU member Erica Jong admitted that an NEA grant had helped support the writing of *Fear of Flying*. More recently, Bush's NEA Chair John Frohnmayer began and ended his career with two controversies over NEA-funded writing. In fall 1989, Frohnmayer tried to pull NEA funding from a New York City art show about AIDS, *Witnesses Against Our Vanishing*, because of an essay written by David Wojnarowicz for the show's catalog. And in winter 1992, Bush fired Frohnmayer when the religious Right attacked a poem titled "Wild Thing," by Sapphire, which appeared in *Queer City*, a gay issue of the literary magazine *the portable lower east side*. In recent years, right-wing censorship targets have often been gay, lesbian, and bisexual.

Right-wingers also go after public libraries, public-school libraries, and public-school curricula. Two favorite books of theocratic censors are Michael Wilhoite's *Daddy's Roommate* and *Heather Has Two Mommies*, by NWU member Leslea Newman—both intended for children of gay or lesbian parents. Another book by an NWU member, Anne Brashler's *Getting Jesus in the Mood*, was challenged in Carroll County, MD. Two groups active in these challenges are Concerned Women For America (CWA) and Citizens For Excellence in Education. CWA members sometimes check "objectionable" books out of libraries and simply refuse to return them. Librarians have shown themselves stalwart authors' allies in resisting censorship. School censorship has been more problematic, partly because Pat Robertson's Christian Coalition is trying to control school boards all over the country by electing "stealth" candidates who do not reveal their more controversial political affiliations until after they are elected.

Many who identify themselves on the left are no less censorious than right-wingers. This is nothing new. For example, the "communitarian" thesis—that collective rights should outweigh mere individual rights—is currently in favor with Bill Clinton, but was effectively employed by Josef Stalin. Liberal censorship is most troubling, not because it's more prevalent than right-wing censorship, but because the transition to fascism occurs when Left and Right collaborate on authoritarian solutions to social problems. Liberals usually attack three kinds of speech (1) pornography and other sexually explicit material, (2) depictions of violence, (3) speech they label "hate" speech or "harassment."

"Pornography" is a favorite right-wing target as well. The Right's most vocal allies in suppressing sexually explicit speech have been the *soi disant* feminists Catharine MacKinnon, Andrea Dworkin, and John Stoltenberg. Since 1983, Dworkin and MacKinnon have promoted anti-pornography laws in towns, cities, and state legislatures. Language from their anti-porn bills has been incorporated into Federal legislation as well. They've also waged campaigns against individual books. For example, Rebecca Chalker's *A Woman's Book of Choices* came under attack by Dworkin.

*'Pornography' is a favorite target of Left and Right*

Thus far, whenever a MacKinnon-Dworkin bill has been passed it's been subsequently struck down by the courts. MacKinnon has had more success in Canada, where her arguments were accepted by the Canadian Supreme Court in the 1991 Butler decision. Since then, "harmful" speech has been unprotected in Canada, and the predictable crackdown has been mostly borne by gay, lesbian, bisexual, feminist, and Leftist writers. Books by NWU member John Preston have been banned in Canada. Canada has suppressed works by serious literary and political writers such as Marguerite Duras and African-American feminist bell hooks, as well as by Dworkin herself. Since no American publisher wants to give up the Canadian market, Canadian censorship may limit what can be printed in the U.S.

## Violence Against Violence

MacKinnon's basic argument—that unfettered speech "causes" both oppression and violence—has been appropriated by those wishing to outlaw "hate speech" and "harassment," as well as by those who'd ban depictions of violence. One result has been the proliferation of campus speech codes, championed by such MacKinnon allies as Richard Delgado, Mari Matsuda, Kimberlé Crenshaw, Charles Lawrence, and Stanley Fish. Massachusetts Institute of Technology, for example, has a speech code that defines *harassment* to include "any conduct, *verbal* or physical, on or *off campus*...which creates an intimidating, hostile, or *offensive* educational, work, or living environment." (author's italics) The handbook describing the code asks MIT students to view free speech as an *interest* rather than a right, a chilling position for a world-renowned university to take.

The "bad" speech that liberals are most aggressively attacking is the depiction of violence. Congressional leaders advocating anti-violence censorship are Senators Paul Simon (D-IL), Kent Conrad (D-ND), and Congressman Ed Markey (D-MA). Conrad works with right-wing leaders and groups, such as Terry Rakolta and the National Coalition on Television Violence. Markey has written the "V-chip" legislation, which would require TV sets to include a chip to block all programs coded for violence. Simon previously supported Jesse Helms in trying to ban NEA support of "offensive" (read gay/lesbian) art. (Simon voted for Helms' NEA bill in 1991.) Simon hasn't advertised his support of Helms, who is unpopular with liberals. Simon has, however, obtained enormous media coverage in his battle against depictions of violence on television. He's held news conferences to proclaim: "The evidence is overwhelming that television adds to violence in our society."

Simon and Markey, and others such as Representative Joe Kennedy (D-MA), had been threatening unconstitutional legislation if the networks and cable industry didn't institute self-censorship. Such bullying tactics have worked in the past with both the motion-picture and recording industries. And, predictably, they worked again. On February 1, 1994, Simon held a press conference with representatives of the networks and cable industry to announce that he had got what he wanted.

*The leading censors in the U.S. are those with the power to determine what information gets out: the industry itself*

The "conflict" between the television industry and the government was almost certainly a sham. Media-industry owners have enormous political clout, so no genuine conflict with Congress is credible. The leading censors in this country are those with the *power* to determine what information gets disseminated—the industry itself.

A censor's principle aim is to effect the most heinous censorship of all—self-censorship. As the media-governmental complex becomes more monolithic, writers have the apparent choice of giving the behemoth what it wants and being paid, or of finding other income and resigning themselves to preaching to the converted. All censorship is, in part, economic.

Grim as the prospects appear, I'm not totally pessimistic. First, the media-governmental complex will become more inefficient as it becomes more bloated, and more truth can then slip between the cracks. Secondly, the war for control of the electronic marketplace is far from over, and some very smart people are fighting to keep cyberspace free. (Many, I'm proud to say, are members of the NWU.) And finally, I disagree with Phil Kerby that censorship is the strongest drive in human nature. I'm hopeful that, in the long run, the drive for truth will prove itself stronger.

# Discrimination

## Writers of Color

BY YLEANA MARTINEZ

Writers such as Amy Tan, Alice Walker, and Oscar Hijuelos—whose books have sold millions of copies and been made into movies—shatter the notion of a limited market for works by people of color.

But for every Tan, Walker, or Hijuelos, there are scores of equally talented writers of color—and an undeniable barrier confronting them when it comes to publishing. Based on the reality that the industry remains largely white, writers of color have less access to agents, editors, and other literary gatekeepers.

The NWU sponsored a pilot study, perhaps the first of its kind, to identify writers of color in New England and to document their experiences with publishing. For the project, we identified as writers of color people of African, Latin, Asian, or Native American heritage. Below are some of our findings.

### PUBLISHERS ARE QUICK TO PIGEONHOLE

A consistent theme was the concern that the major players in publishing have preconceptions—stereotypes—about what writers of color can do.

One Puerto Rican man, who writes reviews, poetry, fiction, and essays, pointed to the "assumption that we can only write about Latino stuff. Why do Anglos think we can't write intelligently about Joyce, Bach, or Marcel Duchamp?"

Respondents blamed publishers' assumptions for other types of pigeonholing: encouraging work that might fit with the 'magic realism' of so much Latin literature, but rarely finding space on their lists for works by African-American writers that feature well-educated, middle-class black characters.

An Asian-American woman, a poet and fiction writer, said: "People try to typecast me as a genre writer."

*'People try to typecast me as a genre writer' says an Asian-American poet and fiction writer*

A Hispanic woman who has authored two books and writes poetry, fiction, and essays, agreed. "The industry considers the literature of peoples of color as specialty markets; white writing as universal," she said. "The audience is there, some of it starved for material from their own experience. But publishers, particularly big publishers, are scarce as hen's teeth. Right now, I'm located in a small corner of a small corner: a woman of color in a white feminist publishing world. It feels precarious."

## No Tech Writers (of Color) Need Apply

The problem is evident in areas outside the literary realm. An African-American business and technical writer wrote: "The worlds of business and high tech are notoriously exclusive of women and people of color. Business and technical writing often involve a lot of client contact, and most traditional managers seem uncomfortable with us representing their company." She added: "There's a perception that women and people of color are okay at writing poetry and fiction, but that we're out of our element when it comes to dealing with technical material."

We asked the participants whether they thought the obstacles they perceived were placed intentionally or were due to lack of awareness within the industry about the marketability of their product. All cited lack of awareness — "ignorance," one wrote.

"It is also just due to the clannish nature of publications, and publications in preferring their own bunch," one said. "Racism exists as a barrier, but it's the kind that caters to *exoticism* and *ethnicity*."

A Native American writer and marketing specialist said: "I could not find a publisher for a book about my people. After going to five publishing houses, Syracuse University Press agreed to publish the book. The book is now out of print and is being reprinted."

"They're still not willing to take a chance on new writers," said another. "The perennial complaint has been that many publishing houses on the East Coast prefer to do anthologies of Chicano writing, . . . plucking just those works they want from the larger body of literature these authors might have."

The dearth of writers of color, respondents said, is a result of structural racism in the industry. Writers of color are not "in the loop." For example, a 1993 survey done by the National Association of Hispanic Journalists found that of Hispanics working in newsrooms only 14 percent are managers. The same study found that the total representation of Hispanics among the newsroom staff of the largest circulation newspapers is four percent.

Most editors and agents don't want to deal with anyone who isn't referred by someone they know. "It's hard to meet the heavy hitters in the publishing industry if you don't have common acquaintances and colleagues," said an African-American writer and journalism professor. Another wrote: "We need more black editors in publishing."

Added a third: "They lose because they're turning away from the diversity of reality in this country. And not facing reality is a dangerous thing."

## FINANCIAL OBSTACLES

Almost all writers face financial obstacles at some point in their careers, if not throughout. However, people of color on the average have less inherited wealth and other forms of income that would allow them to dedicate themselves to their writing alone. Also, government-sponsored grants for writers have been reduced to a trickle.

None of the participants supported themselves entirely through their writing. A woman who has been writing fiction and essays for 15 years, said: "I don't write for pay."

An African-American woman poet and playwright said: "The frustration I feel is more related to trying to set up my life and my money so I have more uninterrupted time to focus on my work."

A good number of writers of color start their careers by self-publishing, or with small presses. This presents another hurdle when it comes to marketing their work. Chain stores, the predominant outlet for the bookselling industry, are reluctant to provide shelf space for titles not handled through major distributors.

NWU member Stan Luxenberg, in his report *Books in Chains: Chain Bookstores and Marketplace Censorship*, recognized this as a problem: "Since small press publishers put out many Latin, Native-American and African-American books, these writers are not getting out. Chains often limit titles by black authors to books by celebrities such as Bill Cosby. Most black publishers have stopped trying to sell books to the chains, since they feel it is a waste of sales resources."

"Advocacy is crucial," summarized one writer. "We need more visibility and clout as writers of color. It means building a strong writers union."

# Gay, Lesbian, Bisexual Writers

BY MAX HUNTER

Do writers who are gay, lesbian, bisexual, or of other sexual minority status (GLB writers) face special problems and concerns not shared by writers in general? What can be done to address such problems and concerns?

To explore these questions, the NWU's Boston Local conducted a survey of gay, lesbian, and bisexual writers in 1992. We tried to develop a questionnaire that would elicit very personal and anecdotal responses—and that's what we got.

## NO SHORTAGE OF PROBLEMS OR SUGGESTIONS

Some of the problems identified, along with suggestions for action, follow.

■ While no mainstream publisher today would refuse to publish a book simply because it contains GLB themes, getting a publisher's attention remains difficult. The best results have been achieved by writers who directly approach editors who are themselves gay or lesbian or who have proven receptive to such material, or by writers who work with particularly receptive agents.

- Mainstream publishers seldom promote GLB books as heavily as they do other books, on the assumption that they appeal only to a limited readership. Compounding this, gay publishers—including the several lesbian small presses—usually advertise their books only in gay/lesbian publications. While the GLB readership is a large, dependable, and growing market, publishers have to be persuaded that good writing appeals to all literate readers—if it's brought to their attention.

- The GLB press itself often treats its writers disrespectfully and unprofessionally. Writers, both staff and freelance, are expected to accept poor treatment and poor pay "for the sake of the movement." Among many abuses mentioned are failure to return manuscripts or confer with writers over editorial changes, and payments that are often long delayed or never made.

- Bookstores, especially the chains, are reluctant to carry GLB books, and, when they do, tend to relegate them to obscure gay/lesbian sections. The same is true of many libraries. There is no good reason why gay/lesbian mystery novels or biographies, for example, should not be displayed in the regular mystery and biography sections. The NWU's campaign to induce chain bookstores to carry midlist and more marginal and small press titles is thus of particular importance to GLB writers.

- GLB books, regardless of their importance, are seldom reviewed by major newspapers—which often review non-GLB books of little literary significance.

- Lesbian respondents felt themselves to be particularly disadvantaged. There were several complaints of sexism within the GLB writing community. Both mainstream publishers and the gay press tend to regard the work of lesbians as of less significance, and less economic value, than that of gay male writers.

*One male writer resented editors' presumption that gays can only compose pornography*

- There were complaints concerning editorial expectations of sexual content in GLB writing. One male writer said editors asked for more explicit sex, and he resented the presumption that gay writers only write pornography; a woman complained that some lesbian publishers seemed more interested in sex scenes than in literary quality.

The issue of fair access is a crucial one. Economic and ideological censorship cannot be tolerated. The NWU is committed to advocating for the equal rights of all writers, and we call on all writers to support each other in the struggle for free expression and equitable industry standards.

4

*About the Union*

# The National Writers Union: A History[1]

BY ALEC DUBRO

"You can't organize freelance writers," they said. "They're too isolated, too indivualistic. They don't want a union." Twelve years later, 4,000 National Writers Union members have proven them wrong. Of course, whenever a new group tries to organize a union, someone always comes up with a reason why it won't work.

In 1935, both labor and management told Heywood Broun that you could not organize newspaper reporters, they were too individualistic. But Broun began the Newspaper Guild that year and noted, "The snobbishness of the white-collar groups is on the whole exaggerated. A very considerable proportion of white-collar workers are ready now to join the parade of organization if only space is assigned to them."

But no space was ever assigned to us. American labor law militates against organizing freelancers, considering us to be independent contractors, outside the National Labor Relations Act, and prohibited from bargaining collectively. So in October 1981, we decided to make our own space.

There had been other attempts to organize. In 1921, 350 writers formed the Authors League. But its book and magazine wing, the Authors Guild, quickly abandoned collective bargaining. In the early 1930s, the Communist Party promoted a Writers Union, which had one goal: to create a public-works project for out-of-work writers. When Roosevelt's Federal Writers Project hired 6,000 writers, that union faded.

Since the 1930s, newspaper, screen, TV, and radio writers were organized into the Newspaper Guild, the Writers Guild of America,

[1]Particular thanks to Elliot Negin and Nancy DuVergne Smith for their scholarly articles on the formation of the union. And to John Dinges, Bruce Hartford, Suzanne Gordon, and others for their recollections.

and the American Federation of Television and Radio Artists. But freelance print writers have been suffering since...well, probably since Homer. Matters came to a head in the 1980s for two major reasons: the right-wing threat to freedom of expression and the explosive growth of media conglomerates that enriched owners but not writers.

In fact, in 1979 the Authors Guild had released a study that determined that writers working a minimum of 20 hours a week averaged $4,775 a year. While that figure was contested by publishers, no one disputed that magazine fees were plummeting. In 1960, *Reader's Digest* paid $2,000 for a feature article; in 1980 they paid $2,850. In real dollars, that was a 49 percent drop. If the fee had kept pace with inflation, it would now be $10,095. It is closer to $4,000.

So, the desire of writers to spend a little of their time and money to pressure for industrywide changes was not surprising. What was surprising was that we acted on that desire.

## How It Began

The timing was not great, I will admit. Ronald Reagan had just fired the striking air traffic controllers; union membership was dropping; media coverage of labor was nonexistent; employers were hiring union-busters.

Still, in early 1981, small groups of writers in Boston and New York formed the Organizing Committee for a National Writers Union. Their immediate goal was to place the issue of a union on the agenda of the American Writers Congress. Although the congress organizers were dubious, they agreed.

A room for about 50 was reserved, for a small caucus. But when hundreds showed up, the meeting was moved to Town Hall. The packed house rose in wild applause for the idea of a union, and when the congress was over, activists left with more than 500 names and a little purse of donations. So it began.

At the first national meeting, held in Princeton, New Jersey, in May 1982, it was apparent that the union had a built-in conflict. There were those who favored strong local chapters and those who wanted a centralized organization concentrating on New York and the publishing industry. In writing the constitution, John Dinges, the union's first secretary for organization, worked out the compromise that gave the union a strong national directorate, as well as local autonomy.

Under its first president, novelist Barbara Raskin, OCNWU worked out a structure. The union is run by its delegates, elected proportionally from the locals. The delegates, who meet each year, nominate a national executive board, including a president, secretary-treasurer, and numerous vice-presidents. The NEB oversees the work of the paid national staff and steers the goals made at the delegates assembly.

In the fall of 1982, the OCNWU met again, this time in Brooklyn, New York, ratified the constitution, and changed our name. From then on, we were the National Writers Union. We elected feminist writer Andrea Eagan as the first union president, and started organizing.

## Champagne Goals, a Near-Beer Budget

From the start, the Writers Union faced a difficult problem: How do you organize people whose annual income from their work was frequently far less than that of a minimum-wage job? Simply holding together any organization is costly, and organizing is very costly. We supplemented our dues the old-fashioned way: We begged.

During our first years, the union received money and in-kind donations from other unions: The Communications Workers of America, the International Ladies Garment Workers Union, the United Food & Commercial Workers, United Steelworkers of America, Hotel Workers & Restaurant Workers Union, and others.

Perhaps most important, District 65 of the United Auto Workers in New York donated office space and free copying. For six years, the Writers Union operated out of an overheated 10-by-20-foot office at 13 Astor Place in lower Manhattan. It was not pretty, but it did the job.

We had vowed to rely on the work of members themselves, but they could not process memberships, answer phones daily, cover necessary travel, print or mail documents. Those tasks needed people, and we held it together in New York with part-timers and volunteer help until 1986, when the union hired Kim Fellner, communications director of the Screen Actors Guild, as full-time executive director.

Meanwhile, across the country the union idea was taking root. Locals formed and prospered in Boston, San Francisco, Washington, Chicago, and Westchester County. Others arose in Baltimore, Oklahoma, and Philadelphia, only to struggle and fail. Areas where writers abound, like Los Angeles, did not organize for several years; others, like Minneapolis-St. Paul and Santa Cruz, California, built locals and held on.

*The union's first big win: reclaiming $50,000 in stiffed fees from Larry Flynt*

With support from the locals, the national office was able to provide backup when we went for our first collective-bargaining contracts at *Mother Jones* and *The Nation*. Then, the union proved itself able to fight hostile publishers when in 1984, it took on the *Rebel*, a news magazine owned by Larry Flynt, which had stiffed freelancers more than $50,000. We got the money. Since then, the total of reclaimed fees has risen to nearly $1 million.

By our second annual delegates assembly in Cambridge, Massachusetts, in 1985, we had 1,300 members. And we had handled grievances and contracts, provided support and, perhaps best of all, had built a strong, cohesive group that actually liked to work together.

## Affiliation

But it was also apparent that we faced severe limitations on growth if we did not get some help. When I was elected president in 1987, I wanted to see the NWU affiliate with a larger union, both for resources and even more for reasons of identification. We needed to be more firmly inside the house of labor.

In every other industrialized country, freelance writers are organized by the journalists union. And according to many European writers-union activists, freelancers have little chance of prevailing on their own. "We need the journalists union, even if there are strains between staff writers and freelancers," said one.

We began a series of committees, searches, board meetings, and assemblies. We met with the Newspaper Guild, Writers Guild of America, and two major industrial unions: the Communications Workers of America and District 65 of the UAW.

I left office in 1990, and Jonathan Tasini took over the job. The affiliation issue continued, but argument only proved to strengthen, not destroy, members' resolve to accomplish it.

Then, at the July 1991 assembly, the delegates overwhelmingly approved affiliation to the UAW. The subsequent membership vote came in at 70 percent in favor, 30 percent opposed.

In January 1992, we became Local 1981 (the date of the American Writers Congress) of the UAW.

## Class Struggle in Cyberspace

With greater organizing resources, and the UAW backing us, the union decided to venture into new areas.

While we had previously discussed the issues of concentration of media ownership and computerization, it was not until 1991 that we applied for a grant to study computer databases. What we found confirmed our worst fears: Major publications were reselling articles to companies such as Nexis, Dialog, and others without compensating writers.

In 1993, Tasini and Secretary-Treasurer Bruce Hartford, a computer technical writer, drafted a white paper entitled *Electronic Publishing Issues*. At the 1993 delegates assembly we established a standing New Technologies Committee, and sanctioned support for a lawsuit brought by the union against Nexis and a series of publishers for unauthorized resale of articles.

The lawsuit was only part of a broad strategy to make writers players in the evolving legal and legislative battles over technology. As Tasini and Hartford wrote, "If we remain silent on the sidelines, the rules, practices, and customs of the new electronic marketplaces will be determined entirely by publishers and vendors for their benefit and not ours."

The union has come a long way from a group of aggrieved writers reaching for power. We are on the way to equity at the workplace, and none too soon. As Jonathan Tasini has said, "We have to be the leading organization for writers in the United States, the one that takes the risks."

At the moment, there seems to be little doubt of that.

# Grievances

BY BRETT HARVEY

By the time you read this, the National Writers Union will have won a total of $1 million for writers through its grievance procedure. The Union's grievance system is unique in the publishing world because the NWU is the only writers organization that handles grievances for its members. And it's unique in the world of organized labor because it has been specifically designed to meet the particular needs and work situations of freelance writers. The system depends on simple, effective procedures that have been distilled from an innovative combination of common sense, creative combativeness, and a growing body of experience.

A grievance is really nothing more than a claim of injustice by a writer, and the Union's agreement to support that claim. A grievance can arise from a contract violation (written or oral), failure to pay, abuse of copyright, or any number of other more complex and subtle disputes. Book grievances, for example, may involve unwanted editorial changes in a manuscript, withholding of royalties, or failure to publish within a specified time limit. Magazine grievances most often entail late payments, kill fee disputes and, in recent years, copyright violations.

The grievance procedure itself couldn't be simpler. First, the writer herself writes the publisher or editor clearly stating the problem, setting a deadline for redress, and threatening to turn to the NWU if she doesn't receive satisfaction. Most potential grievances are resolved at this stage—before they even become grievances, in other words. If satisfaction isn't received by the deadline, the NWU grievance officer steps in and writes the offending publisher on the writer's behalf. Sometimes a few followup calls are needed, but 80 percent of the time, this letter does the trick. The grievance officer consults with the writer at every stage and does only what she is comfortable with.

No problem should be considered too small—or too large, for that matter—to become a grievance. The $1 million won by the NWU consists of a multitude of kinds and sizes of problems, from the $25 owed a writer by a neighborhood newspaper, to the $3,000 fee a pharmaceutical publications firm tried to renege on when its client canceled the contract.

Here are some other true stories from the NWU's grievance annals:

- A freelancer hands in an assigned piece to her editor at a major women's magazine. Weeks go by with no word from the editor as to its fate. After a month, the editor calls and asks for a rewrite. The writer complies and hands it in. Another six weeks go by. When the writer calls her editor, she is told that "the piece is fine, really good, and I'm passing it on to the editor-in-chief." A month later, the editor calls to tell the writer that the piece has been killed. The explanation? "We have a new editor-in-chief, and she's taking the magazine in a different direction, so we won't be using this kind of piece anymore." In spite of the writer's protests, the editor refuses to offer more than a 20 percent kill fee. The NWU steps in and argues that the writer had not been dealt with in a timely or respectful manner, that her piece had been held for an unconscionably long time, and that it had been killed for reasons unrelated to the quality of the work. In other words, the writer has fulfilled her part of the contract and should be paid in full. After a series of letters and phone calls, the magazine agrees to pay the full fee.

- An experienced science writer signs a book contract with an established publisher. Because the subject is complex, the publisher insists the manuscript be sent to a series of outside reviewers. Each new reviewer makes a different set of comments, many of them contradictory, forcing the author to do numerous rewrites. Ultimately, the publisher rejects the manuscript and demands repayment of the author's advance. The NWU gets the publisher to agree to accept a greatly reduced amount, to be repaid only when the author receives a new advance from another publisher.

■ A medical writer contracts to do a series of 10 articles for a major health magazine, for a fee of $10,000. The pieces are to be vetted by the American Medical Association. The writer completes the series, his editor expresses satisfaction, and he is paid—but only for eight of the pieces. The reasons are unclear, but evidently have to do with problems that have developed between the magazine and the AMA, as well as space considerations. The magazine refuses to pay the last $2,000, arguing—well after the pieces have been accepted for publication—that the articles were unsatisfactory. When the writer's attempts to get satisfaction fail, he turns to the Union. The NWU points out that the writer's contract called for payment on acceptance by the magazine's editors and was not contingent on approval by the AMA, that his work had been accepted by the magazine, and he should be paid in full. He is.

■ A poet submits a poem to a small literary magazine in the South, answering an ad that promises a subscription as payment for anything they publish. She never hears from them, but comes across a copy of the magazine months later, which includes a badly edited version of her poem, with words added and lines broken differently from the original. She receives no answer to her written complaint. The NWU writes the editors demanding an apology, a reprint of the poem as written in a future issue, and the promised subscription to the magazine. The editors acknowledge their mistake and promise to redress it.

*From an unwanted editorial change in a magazine to withheld book royalties, grievances can be won*

Every time a writer brings a grievance against a publisher, he is educating that publisher (and often himself as well) about what constitutes fair and respectful treatment. By the same token, it could be said that every time a writer lets a publisher get away with abusing him, he's making it harder for all writers. Each time the National Writers Union successfully intervenes on behalf of a writer, it strengthens not only the writer, but the union itself—which, in turn, enhances its power and effectiveness in the industry. And each time the NWU wins a grievance, it sends a message to the industry that writers, acting together, are a force to be reckoned with.

# NWU *Organizing &* *Membership Benefits*

**NWU MEMBERSHIP CARD:**
Members receive a union card, certifying they are members in good standing of the National Writers Union/UAW Local 1981.

*The Standard Journalism Contract is on page 61.*

**STANDARD JOURNALISM CONTRACT:**
The NWU offers members its Standard Journalism Contract and supports its use through training and handbooks.

*See page 193 for more details on grievance procedures.*

**GRIEVANCES:**
The Union's local and national grievance committees help members resolve disputes with publishers.

**CAMPAIGNS:**
The NWU's Journalism, Book, and Electronic Publishing Campaigns work to educate writers and to advocate for writers' rights in these three areas.

**INSURANCE:**
All members in good standing are eligible to participate in the NWU major medical plan, which offers comprehensive coverage, regardless of pre-existing conditions, age, or sex.

**NWU GUIDE TO BOOK CONTRACTS:**
The Union publishes a detailed guide to book contracts, which includes advice on and model language for all major clauses of a publishing contract.

**PREFERRED LITERARY AGENT AGREEMENT:**
The NWU offers members a model agent contract, which is accompanied by a detailed guide.

**AGENTS DATABASE:**

The Union's agents database offers a realistic perspective on agents, based on the experiences of NWU members.

**JOB BANKS:**

Several locals operate formal job banks, as well as providing access to more informal networks.

**EVENTS:**

Locals regularly offer seminars, panels, and parties.

**POLITICAL ACTIVISM:**

Through its Political Issues Committee, the NWU informs members and advocates on their behalf.

**PRESS PASS:**

The Union certifies members as working journalists and issues press credentials.

**PUBLICATIONS:**

The NWU continuously prepares and makes available a variety of useful and topical publications— e.g., "Books in Chains," "A Writer's Guide to the Internet," "Electronic Publishing Issues," "Negotiating Your Electronic Rights: Guidelines for Journalists," "Contracts Between Writers and Electronic Book Publishers," and many others.

In addition, the union publishes *American Writer*, a magazine for members.

The local chapters also publish newsletters and other materials.

**DISCOUNTS:**

For car rentals, health plans, delivery service, etc.

# Contributors

**Robert B. Chatelle**'s published fiction includes short stories in literary magazines and erotic stories for gay men. His nonfiction addresses issues of free expression and personal freedom, especially for sexual minorities. He currently serves the NWU as Political Issues Chair and is a former member of the National Executive Board.

**Alec Dubro** sold his first article to *Rolling Stone* in 1968 and received a harsh awakening: "The subject's career took off, the magazine prospered, and I got $15." A member of the Union since 1982, he served as national President from 1987 to 1990. He is currently chair of the DC local and still freelancing. But, he says, "Now I won't go for a penny under $20."

**Frank Free** is National Grievance Officer of the NWU, and a former Western Region Vice President and Co-Chair of the Bay Area local. His first novel, *Fly From Evil*, was published in 1986; his column, "Mot Juste," appears in MediaFile. He lives in Berkeley, CA, and practices law.

**Alex Halberstadt** is a writer living in New York City. His work appears in *ZYZZYVA, Artforum,* and *Monumental Propaganda*. He is a curator at ArtSpace, an electronic arts center.

**Bruce Hartford** is Secretary-Treasurer of the NWU. Formerly a freelance journalist, he has been a freelance technical writer in Silicon Valley for the past fourteen years for companies such as Apple, Sun, Borland, and others.

**Brett Harvey** is a journalist and children's book writer whose most recent book, *The Fifties: A Women's Oral History*, has recently been published in paperback by HarperCollins. She serves as Eastern Regional Grievance Officer of the National Writers Union.

**Max Hunter**, a resident of Key West and a long-time NWU activist, is a novelist whose most recent book, *The Final Bell*, was released by Alyson Publications.

**Alexander Kopelman** is a New York writer. He is currently working on a historical nonfiction book.

**David Lida**'s journalism has been published in national magazines for more than a decade. "Freelancing from Afar" is adapted from a memoir he is writing about his experiences in Mexico.

**Judith Levine** is the author of *My Enemy, My Love: Women, Men, and the Dilemmas of Gender* (Anchor/1993) and a journalist who has written on gender, race, and social issues for many national publications, including *Vogue*, *Columbia Journalism Review*, *Harper's Bazaar*, and the *Village Voice*. She is a founder of the National Writers Union.

**Yleana Martinez**, of Cambridge, Mass., is a freelancer who writes about travel and folk culture. She is currently writing a novel.

**Philip Mattera** is the NWU's National Book Grievance Officer and Co-Chair of the union's New Technologies campaign. He is the author of four books on economics, business and labor, and he does research on corporations for labor unions.

**Catherine Revland** has published 24 trade books, many of them in collaboration. She has just finished her first novel.

**Kathryn Shagas** is a graphic designer who lives in Glyndon, Maryland.

**Jonathan Tasini** is President of the National Writers Union. He has been a freelance journalist specializing in labor and economics for more than a decade. He is currently working on a book for W.W. Norton on the global economy.

**Charles Thiesen**, a long-time NWU activist, has been Chair of the Boston local and External Organizing Vice President of the union. A former freelance journalist, he works as a technical writer in Boston to support his novel-writing habit.

**Keith Watson** is a Chicago-based writer and editor specializing in corporate communications for service industries and professional organizations. Formerly a TV columnist and arts-and-entertainment writer for *The Houston Post*, he has served for two years as voluntary chair of the NWU's Chicago local.

# Index